THE B2B MARKETING REVOLUTION

A BATTLE PLAN FOR GUARANTEED OUTCOMES

LORI TURNER-WILSON

The B2B Marketing Revolution™:
A Battle Plan for Guaranteed Outcomes

www.marketingresultsguaranteed.com
www.b2bmarketingrevolution.com
www.marketingtoolsforyou.com
www.loriturnerwilson.com

Published by Made to Change the World™ Publishing
Nashville, Tennessee

Cover and interior designed by Chelsea Jewell

ISBN: 978-1-956837-32-2
ISBN: 978-1-956837-34-6

Printed in the USA, Canada, Australia, and Europe

"*The B2B Marketing Revolution*™ distills complex marketing challenges into a clear, actionable framework for success. An essential read for leaders seeking strong, predictable marketing outcomes."

— GINO WICKMAN, AUTHOR OF *TRACTION* AND *SHINE*, CREATOR OF EOS®

"*The B2B Marketing Revolution*™ provides leaders with battle-tested, research-based, and actionable strategies, plans, and tools to win the war for customers in an increasingly competitive marketplace."

— BUCK BROWN, PRESIDENT AND CEO, iSCREEN VISION

"Lori is a marketing genius with the reputation to prove it. In *The B2B Marketing Revolution*™, she reveals her winning philosophy and teaches the ROI-driving marketing strategies that help brand executives unlock unprecedented revenue and ignite teams to excel. This is the one resource every B2B leader should have."

— LEE HARRIS, MAYOR OF SHELBY COUNTY, TN

"I found this book to be truly revolutionary from the importance of marketing research, to having a scalable marketing plan, to partnering with an agency offering a guaranteed return on investment. The decreased concerns about performance of a marketing plan, having accountability, and the ability to better predict growth makes this the book of the decade!!"

— J.W. GIBSON, II, CEO AND CHAIRMAN, GIBSON COMPANIES

"*The B2B Marketing Revolution*™ sets a new precedent for accountability in marketing. A revolutionary blueprint for leaders tired of the status quo."

— BENTLY GOODWIN, MASTER CHAIR, VISTAGE INTERNATIONAL

"*The B2B Marketing Revolution*™ is essential reading for executive leadership. Our enterprise has always contended that 50 percent of our marketing dollars were well spent. We just never knew which 50 percent were successful. Lori Turner-Wilson provides clarity on how to partner with an agency to build a results-guaranteed marketing strategy. Marketing dollars are then transformed from a nebulous expense item to an investment in your company's future success with a measurable return."

— JACK SAMMONS, PRESIDENT, AMPRO INDUSTRIES

"We live in a time where innovation is happening all around us, but we have not seen a radical shift in the approach to marketing until now. *The B2B Marketing Revolution*™ brings us a framework that clearly defines a profound formula for results guaranteed, something every business leader wants and needs."

— GLENN MALONE, OWNER, WELLENGOOD PARTNERS

"*The B2B Marketing Revolution*™ is a bright light in the world of marketing. The use of deep research and analytics to drive high-performance, innovative marketing strategies is changing the way firms are leveraging their marketing capital to attain remarkable results. This book is a true marketing revolution."

— CHUCK HOGAN, CO-FOUNDER, YOUR BEST LIFE

"*The B2B Marketing Revolution*™ calls for a radical re-evaluation of what businesses should demand from marketing. This book details the steps required and delivers a manifesto for industry change."

— ROB DAVIES, CEO, STEALTH-ISS

"As an owner of 18 businesses, I've seen enough jargon-filled advice to last a lifetime. Lori's book is different. It's like having a conversation with a friend who just happens to be a B2B marketing genius. She turns the whole game on its head, simplifying what others complicate and laying out a clear path to success with B2B marketing."

— PRESTON BROWN, CEO, ZIA HOMES

To all the middle-market B2B leaders in this world fighting to make a difference in the lives of their employees and customers and struggling to realize the kind of growth they see so clearly in their vision. To those entrepreneurial heroes carrying the weight of company performance and the sleepless nights. To those ready to torch what's not working to build what does. This book is for you.

CONTENTS

ACKNOWLEDGMENTS

My marketing career has required resilience and dogged determination, qualities deeply rooted in the support and unwavering faith of my parents, Chuck and Rita Turner. Watching my father ascend from a tire salesman to senior leadership and finally to the entrepreneur he always dreamt he'd be instilled in me a profound respect for the importance of authentic relationship building and the kind of dynamic leadership and drive that inspires others to action. His example taught me to lean into my intuition, to stand resolute in the face of difficult decisions, to work until the job is done right, to have an insatiable desire to learn, and to cultivate unyielding tenacity. His legacy is one of infectious enthusiasm, warmth, and humor; if bottled, it would have changed the world. Despite the challenges in his day, and there were many, he had an innate ability to leave his troubles at the office and not burden his family. Dad, I'm still working on this one. Even though his voice was silenced prematurely by cancer, his wisdom continues to guide me.

My mom, the unwavering pillar of integrity, instilled in me a moral compass that insists on the highest standards and a commitment to always do the right thing. She nurtured an ambition that was invisible to my own eyes, believing in my potential before I could even conceive of it. When I wondered if something was possible, I'd look to her. The answer was always "yes." Her steadfast presence has been a guiding light directing me toward my aspirations. In fact, most of my accomplishments can be directly linked to the faith she has always had in me. Together, my parents have been the architects of my character and the silent partners in every success I have achieved.

Moreover, my younger siblings, Staci and Andrew, whose infectious humor and spirit remind me to not take life too seriously, have added balance to my journey.

Shortly before we lost our father, I met Mike—the person who would soon become my anchor. It was a blessing that my father got to see the beginning of what Mike would mean to me. He is my cornerstone; he holds my world together. Leading a company can be like riding a rollercoaster without a restraint—something he knows firsthand—and his humor is a tonic when I need it most. His support is unwavering, and his encouragement is my fuel. If not for Mike driving me around the country in our RV, I doubt these words would have ever made it onto the pages. He knew the road is where I do my best thinking and creating, and it's where this book came to life.

RedRover's story probably would have never moved beyond an idea if not for Julie, my co-conspirator in entrepreneurship. Side by side, we took the leap to start RedRover. Those formative times in our scant 700-square-foot office space were as challenging as they were rewarding, and they remain some of my fondest memories. I'm immensely grateful for the friendship and shared dedication that Julie brought to our venture from day one. Thanks for the memories and for being an integral part of this journey.

I am deeply grateful to the members of my Vistage Memphis and Tampa peer CEO groups. Your clear-eyed perspectives, radical candor, accountability, and friendships have been invaluable as I've navigated RedRover's expansion. A heart-felt thank you to each of you: Tampa—Janice, John, Rob, Sabina, Eug, Matt, Brent, Luis, Amber, and Ron; Memphis—Bently, Brandon, Henry, Buck, Larry, Brian, Rusty, Douglas, Michael, Scott, Kirk, Carmon, Phillip, Mitch, Joe, Rob, Greg, and Doug. Doug, your knack for cutting through the noise has often provided clarity in the most challenging situations, particularly your timely "you know what to do" reminders that I usually have the answers if I just tune in.

My dear friend Tammie has been an integral part of the RedRover journey, offering clarity when my path seems obscured. Her own journey as a writer has inspired me on the days when creativity seems just out of reach. But it's her effortless humor that I value the most. A life with laughter is a life well spent, and with Tammie, it's always well spent.

And I am grateful to my fellow pack members at RedRover who inspire me daily with their impressive talent, tireless dedication, and desire to win for our clients. While this book is inspired by our entire pack and their unrelenting pursuit of excellence, a special thanks goes to Jee, Juli, and Ashley for their specific contributions to this book's content.

As I embarked on the ambitious journey of establishing the Memphis Chapter of the American Marketing Association in its inaugural year, I was fortunate to have the support of Russ Klein. As CEO of the national American Marketing Association for seven years and former Global President of Burger King, Russ's guidance was pivotal. His extensive leadership experience, including roles as CMO for Arby's and 7-Eleven, fostered a dynamic collaboration that was instrumental in our chapter's development.

I also have a deep appreciation for Gino Wickman, author of *Traction*; it is this entrepreneurial operating system that has guided the growth and expansion of my company.

While charting my course, I have found rich inspiration in industry icons—Steve Jobs, Neil Patel, Seth Godin, Guy Kawasaki, and Daniel Kahneman. Jobs' transformative approach to product marketing, Patel's genius in digital marketing and analytics, Godin's philosophies on the power of targeting the smallest viable audience and how trust and tension create forward motion, Kawasaki's innovative strategies in brand evangelism, and Kahneman's insightful contributions to behavioral economics and consumer decision making, have all greatly influenced my perspective on what it takes to generate predictable marketing outcomes. Their groundbreaking work has not only revolutionized the field but also provided me with critical insights in my quest to build a framework for predictable marketing outcomes.

FOREWORD

It was 2014, when I was appointed chair of the American Marketing Association (AMA) and looking to share my knowledge and experience through that role, that I met Lori Turner-Wilson, and we, together, launched the Memphis chapter of the AMA. Lori then became the first president of that newly-founded chapter. I knew the chapter was in good hands because even before there was an AMA Memphis, I was aware of Lori's firm, RedRover Sales & Marketing Strategy, as one of the more credentialled and reputed firms in the middle-market B2B arena. And over this last decade, Lori has not only grown RedRover into a national firm, she has made waves with her personal commitment to leveling up middle-market B2B marketing strategies based on comprehensive market research that can be leveraged to ensure predictable marketing ROI outcomes. Like me in 2014, Lori is at a point in her career where she feels compelled to give back and share her insights.

With *The B2B Marketing Revolution*™*: A Battle Plan for Guaranteed Outcomes*, she does just that—she demystifies what has been part of her own success to give CEOs and marketing leaders the chance to build on that knowledge, applying her insights to take their companies to the next level. It perfectly illustrates my personal mantra: knowledge is not power; power is knowledge shared.

So, what knowledge is Lori sharing?

That clients can and should demand guaranteed marketing ROI. I concur. Even without knowing precisely the details of a given guarantee, the very idea of it reflects a self-assuredness that a client wants to see in the people who are giving it guidance and counsel. It's a projection of confidence that marketers can bring to their projections and, thus, their recommendations.

To further the commitment to guaranteeing marketing ROI, Lori proposes that earnings be tied to actual achievements … that there be financial incentives to achieving projected marketing ROI. Again, I concur. This thinking aligns with my ethos that everybody that I do business with prospers. It's only right to be worried about clients' profitability, too. As Lori says, "At the end of the day, as marketers, if we aren't willing to stand behind our own projected outcomes, why the hell are we in this business?" The best way to handle the care and feeding of clients is to allow them to prosper with your success.

Lori also illustrates how the B2B space, particularly in middle-market firms, represents a ripe opportunity for the role of disciplined and accountable marketing. She battles the traditional idea that it's too difficult to measure marketing performance. Instead, she shows CEOs and marketing leaders how their teams, indeed, are capable of achieving the particular dynamic of attributing and ascribing performance down to each touchpoint in a mathematical context because they are armed with analytics and attribution tools. In essence, she proves to the marketers themselves that they can provide projected outcomes and feel confident guaranteeing them. Ultimately, Lori throws down the gauntlet and challenges marketers to either explain how they know what they're doing or why they don't.

Throughout the book, Lori discusses a lot of relevant tensions that are in the mind of the B2B leader, and, in that sense, the book offers some psychotherapy. A CEO or marketing head can read about the battles she describes and go, "I'm wrestling over this issue, too." It's very relatable.

The B2B Marketing Revolution™ is, overall, an elegant construct of concise organizing principles under which Lori's mastery of B2B marketing delivers a playbook for any middle-market business leader.

She uses an "order of battle" approach that resonates and is easy to follow. Each "battle" captures a universal tension that exists inside the mind of every B2B leader, discharged by actionable insights for victory. The content glides for effortless consumption. Bottom line: *The B2B Marketing Revolution*™ answers not just the "What," but the "So what" and the "Now what."

I've found that the best books on marketing teach sound principles and tell a story that is relatable, that is coherent, and that somebody knows what to do with—they create value as a result of having read them. And this most certainly applies to *The B2B Marketing Revolution*™. It has a pragmatism that's lacking in a lot of marketing books, and I think that's why it's a useful playbook for a CEO or marketing leader to keep on their desk.

As a B2C expert, I can wholeheartedly attest that Lori's would be one of the first books I'd reach for if I was asked to consult a B2B client.

— RUSS KLEIN, FORMER CEO AMERICAN MARKETING ASSOCIATION, GLOBAL PRESIDENT BURGER KING, CMO FOR 7-ELEVEN, DR PEPPER/7UP, ARBY'S, AND FCB WORLDWIDE HEAD OF GATORADE ADVERTISING

JOIN THE REVOLUTION. DEFY THE APATHY THE INDUSTRY EXPECTS OF YOU AND DECLARE, "I DESERVE GUARANTEED MARKETING OUTCOMES, AND ANYONE STANDING IN MY WAY WILL BE LOVINGLY REMOVED."

LORI TURNER-WILSON

PREFACE: THE AGONY THAT IS DRIVING AN INDUSTRY TRANSFORMATION

The Beginning

I spent the first 11 years of my career serving in various leadership roles in marketing in the Fortune 1000 world. In these roles, I had the opportunity to hire several of the top 10 advertising agencies in the country. They were wildly creative, without a doubt, and shockingly uninterested in being held accountable to the metrics that actually mattered, such as incremental gross profit. I had P&L accountability, so it stood to reason that the agencies that supported my team would also embrace similar accountability. I soon realized that they were more interested in reach, frequency, and impressions—none of which were on my scorecard. Dragging these agencies into peak performance was agonizing. If you've ever hired agencies or led internal marketing teams, I'm sure you can relate. Somewhere, deep within myself, an idea was percolating—a vision of an agency that was in perfect alignment with my passion for driving bottom-line growth. I continued working side-by-side with various agencies encouraging them to level up their research capabilities and both set and stand behind their projected outcomes. I pushed that boulder uphill until 2003.

The Beginning of the End

It was the beginning of the end of my career in enterprise marketing. "Bring your strategic marketing experience into our internal communications team and use it to drive the kinds of outcomes internally—with employee satisfaction—that you're known for externally." That was the hook that got me to leave the hospitality industry for banking.

During my time in the hospitality and food and beverage industries, I'd built a career on leveraging data to drive measurable marketing outcomes. In fact, I led the team that created TCBY Enterprises' first website. At Hilton Hotel Corporation, I routinely conducted massive 50+ variant direct-mail and email-marketing split testing. My job was to dig deep into the analytics, at a time when this was still a difficult task given the limited capabilities of digital reporting, to uncover the combination of content, imagery, placement, offer, and audience segmentation that would deliver the strongest outcomes— outcomes that I could predict. This was a company that, rightfully so, placed enormous value on customer data insights and exhaustive market research.

The thought of allowing deep data analysis to inform what was essentially an internal marketing strategy fascinated me. I envisioned a ground-breaking employee culture that so rivaled others it served as an unbeatable brand differentiator. So I took the leap!

It was only six months before I realized that, despite the best intentions of some banks, the broader banking industry was not ready for the kind of change I envisioned bringing to internal marketing. Compared to the dynamic hospitality industry, banking felt far more cautious and measured in its approach. I was unable to make the big innovative moves needed to effect real change. The realization hit home during a conversation with a colleague on the leadership team regarding the Creative Director seat I was about to recruit for my team. She asked, "Are you sure Creative Director is the right title? You know we're not really very creative around here. You might be setting the wrong expectation." It was a moment of clarity for me: It was time for me to leave enterprise marketing, where decision making is complex and, thus, progress can be slow, and instead work for smaller companies that are hungry and eager to change—an environment more aligned with my drive for innovation and outcomes.

The Revolution

As I contemplated the next chapter in my life, I imagined an agency that cared as much about the bottom line as I did—one that could move nimbly and effect the growth trajectory of a company rapidly and efficiently by building strategy on a backbone of comprehensive market research. It dawned on me that I should build what I couldn't find and raise the bar in the industry that I loved along the way.

And so, in 2006, RedRover Sales & Marketing Strategy was born.

Over the next 18 years with hundreds of clients, my team and I worked to perfect our approach to hone market research that drives effective and efficient marketing strategies that deliver predictable outcomes across a wide variety of industries—eventually guaranteeing those outcomes for clients. While our work at RedRover is principally B2B, or business-to-business, focused (our clients generally sell to other businesses and not to end consumers), the principles apply in the B2C, or business-to-consumer, world as well. This work, supported by the pioneering research study detailed next in the Introduction, informs a proven framework for developing and executing a results-guaranteed marketing strategy that any company with a compelling value proposition and decent margins can leverage as their battle plan for success. It's called the 12 Battles™ Framework.

Through the years, my team and I have worked with hundreds of clients who were sitting where you likely are today—dissatisfied with the return on their marketing investment, unsure of what's really paying off, frustrated with the inability to accurately predict growth, and wishing their marketing partner would focus on metrics that actually matter.

Our RedRover team has been perfecting our framework for guaranteed marketing ROI (MROI) for 18 years, and we've guaranteed it for the last 4. Now I'm sharing our secrets with middle-market B2B leaders across the country so that you, too, can course-correct your marketing efforts to ensure marketing consistently generates predictable growth at a strong return and becomes a true competitive advantage.

In this book, I'll pull back the curtain and share with you, whether you are a CEO or a marketing leader (or perhaps one in the same), what it takes to build a results-guaranteed marketing plan, one that is proven and predictable—a framework that, up until now, has been confidential.

So why share these trade secrets now? There comes a point in your life when the individual wins become far less important than the impact you leave on the world. I'm tired of seeing middle-market companies waste money on marketing strategies that, frankly, aren't worth the paper they're printed on. I know, from watching my father, what it's like for an owner or senior leader to carry the weight of company performance. I've known it all my life. I saw how hard he worked not to bring that pressure and anxiety home to his family because he didn't want us to have to carry that burden too. Despite his best attempts, though, we knew it was there. What I unequivocally know now is that with the right marketing strategy, any middle-market company can effectively compete with its much larger competitors—easing the burden on those at the helm. Evening the scales for you is my passion. When you win, I'm helping my father and others like him.

While I still create and execute results-guaranteed marketing strategies for my RedRover clients every day, I also want to arm those that want to do it themselves with the knowledge and skills to succeed.

As a CEO or marketing leader, you likely have adopted some preconceived beliefs about marketing either from personal experience or from others' experiences that, over time, have become deeply ingrained. The path to success requires new thinking; you must identify, challenge, and adjust these beliefs. In fact, there are 12

Battles™ in mindset that you must win before you can successfully execute a results-guaranteed marketing plan. Are you ready to oust your current thinking; disrupt how you lead your marketing team; and overthrow how you craft a marketing strategy and, ultimately, how you perform?

12 BATTLES™ FRAMEWORK

1 YOU **ACCEPT** THAT YOU DESERVE AND WILL ACHIEVE GUARANTEED MARKETING OUTCOMES.

2 YOU **ACKNOWLEDGE** THAT YOU DON'T REALLY KNOW THY CUSTOMER.

3 YOU **CHAMPION** MARKET RESEARCH AS A DO-OR-DIE INVESTMENT.

4 YOU **EMBRACE** THE POWER OF ATTRIBUTION MODELING AND STOP ACCEPTING BAD DATA.

5 YOU **OWN** AN OPENING IN THE BRANDSCAPE.

6 YOU **TORCH** YOUR EXISTING STRATEGY UNAPOLOGETICALLY IF NEEDED.

7 YOU **ADVOCATE** FOR AN INVESTMENT IN EACH STAGE OF THE CUSTOMER JOURNEY.

8 YOU **CHALLENGE** YOUR TEAM TO MAKE POWERFUL STRATEGIC SHIFTS GROUNDED IN RESEARCH VERSUS TRADITION.

9 YOU **PREACH** THE GOOD WORD OF DISCIPLINED OPTIMIZATION.

10 YOU **COMMIT** TO BUILDING A PAY-FOR-PERFORMANCE TEAM AROUND YOUR STRATEGY; NOT VICE VERSA.

11 YOU **REQUIRE** A POWERFUL MARKETING DASHBOARD AND DOCUMENTED PROCESSES.

12 YOU **INSPIRE** YOUR TEAM TO STAND BEHIND THEIR MROI PROJECTIONS.

CHECK OUT THE 12 BATTLES™ READER HUB at marketingtoolsforyou.com for this free resource:

12 BATTLES™ FRAMEWORK DOWNLOADABLE CARD

You will only succeed in executing a results-guaranteed marketing plan when you achieve victory in these 12 critical areas—each of which I'm going to break down for you in the chapters that follow.

CHECK OUT THE 12 BATTLES™ READER HUB at marketingtoolsforyou.com for this free resource:

12 BATTLES™ READINESS ASSESSMENT

INTRODUCTION : PIONEERING B2B RESEARCH FOR BENCHMARKING YOUR PERFORMANCE

Why the Research Matters

My team and I have worked with hundreds of clients over RedRover's 18 years in a whole host of industry verticals, proving our 12 Battles™ Framework works in the for-profit B2B space regardless of industry. This framework does not work consistently in the nonprofit space as decisions are not as outcome-driven as they naturally are in for-profit companies, and understandably so. We also know that the model isn't as effective in enterprise-size companies due to the slow nature of decision making and action. The sweet spot is with middle-market B2B companies—especially those in the lower end of middle-market—those with roughly between $10M and $150M in annual revenue. From experience, I have observed that these companies tend to have both pace and simplicity in decision making coupled with the capital to make substantial investments toward their marketing.

To further substantiate our years of in-the-trenches experience, RedRover sponsored a ground-breaking research study of middle-market CEOs and senior marketing leaders across the U.S. called the "2024 RedRover U.S. Middle-Market B2B Marketing Performance Study." With a response rate of more than 400 participants (which is rarely achieved with senior leadership as a target audience in companies of this size), this study has a 95 percent confidence level and a 5 percent margin of error—making it the most substantial body of modern research in the B2B marketing space of its kind. Twenty-two percent of respondents were CEOs; 61 percent were VPs or directors of marketing; and the remaining 17 percent were other C-Suite executives—VPs or directors of sales or VPs of operations. All respondents represented companies between $10M and $150M in annual revenue that invested at least $25,000 a year in marketing.

Middle-market executives in B2B companies have historically found relevant marketing metrics very difficult to come by. This study offers unprecedented access to important KPIs (key performance indicators) needed to both measure and drive marketing performance. I have used these findings to augment what RedRover offers its clients as well as to support the principles in this book.

The link between marketing investment and business growth has never been more evident. Nearly half of middle-market companies dedicate more than 4 percent of their revenue to marketing efforts. This trend underscores a collective acknowledgment of marketing's pivotal role in scaling operations and enhancing competitiveness. However, amidst substantial spending, a surprising number of companies remain in the dark about the exact impact of their marketing dollars and the role that research insights could play in improving their marketing plan performance.

Many companies believe that market research is too expensive an endeavor to execute at the middle-market level when, in reality, it's too expensive not to. The data shows lukewarm satisfaction with marketing performance as a result.

In the Executive Summary that follows, you'll find the most significant of the research findings including marketing spend, MROI, CAC (customer acquisition cost), and LTV (lifetime value of a customer) benchmarks that you can use to gauge your company's performance. You'll learn what market research efforts companies are investing most in, how satisfied they are with their MROI, and how often they're optimizing their marketing strategies for peak performance. There are also never-before-seen insights into how few middle-market companies work with an agency offering a perfor-mance guarantee, why they believe so few agencies offer performance guarantees, why company leadership believes its marketing teams aren't able to better predict outcomes, and how many companies have performance-based compensation plans in place for their marketing team. And you'll learn how scalable, repeatable, and predictable most marketing plans in the middle-market space really are.

This book is organized around the 12 Battles™ Framework, with a chapter per battle. At the end of each chapter, you'll find a recap of the most relevant research insights for that particular chapter. In those recaps, you'll be reminded of the pertinent research from the Executive Summary while also being introduced to additional survey data—often a deeper look at the research including more detailed data cuts.

Following are the most pivotal survey findings and analysis, beginning with a brief overview.

CHECK OUT THE 12 BATTLES™ READER HUB at marketingtoolsforyou.com for this free resource:

2024 REDROVER U.S. MIDDLE-MARKET B2B MARKETING PERFORMANCE STUDY

Executive Summary[1]

Most middle-market B2B companies earn a $3:$1 or $4:$1 MROI. According to the responses, leadership is satisfied, but not highly satisfied, with that MROI. Moreover, most companies work with an agency partner to generate that performance. While satisfaction rises when the agency partner guarantees MROI, most B2B

---

[1] Percentages may be off slightly due to rounding. For more comprehensive research findings, visit marketingtoolsforyou.com.

companies do not partner with one that offers a performance guarantee of any kind. And yet when selecting a future agency partner, leadership cites performance accountability and marketing guarantees as the top two factors that will drive that decision.

So why don't senior leaders actually demand performance accountability and guarantees?

Most senior leaders cite the degree of market competition as the primary reason that they believe marketing teams (whether internal or external) are unable to predict outcomes. Consequently, while they agree that they definitively would be more likely to partner with an agency that offers a guaranteed MROI, they believe the current overarching industry claim that it's not possible. When asked why they believe most marketing agencies don't offer a results guarantee, respondents answered that it's too risky for the agency and it's impossible to predict marketing outcomes. I would argue that the first is an excuse and the second, a myth. These excuses are what most traditional agencies tell their clients because they are (understandably) nervous about leveling up their accountability and, more importantly, they don't have to because clients do not yet demand it.

> **MIDDLE-MARKET B2B LEADERS: MAKE TODAY THE DAY THAT YOU RAISE YOUR EXPECTATIONS.**

Annual Marketing Investment

The responses received show that nearly half of middle-market B2B companies spend at least 4 percent of revenue annually on marketing; 16 percent spend more than 6 percent. For companies with 501 to 1000 employees, nearly 80 percent invest at least 4 percent of revenue in marketing, and the majority reach marketing investment in the 5 to

6 percent range. This increased spend holds true for companies with 1,000+ employees as well. B2B companies seem to understand the crucial role of marketing and align their dollars accordingly.

Of note: Eleven percent of respondents aren't sure what percent of revenue they invest in marketing! Many B2B companies face this lack of clarity in marketing returns. If you're in that camp, this book can help you.

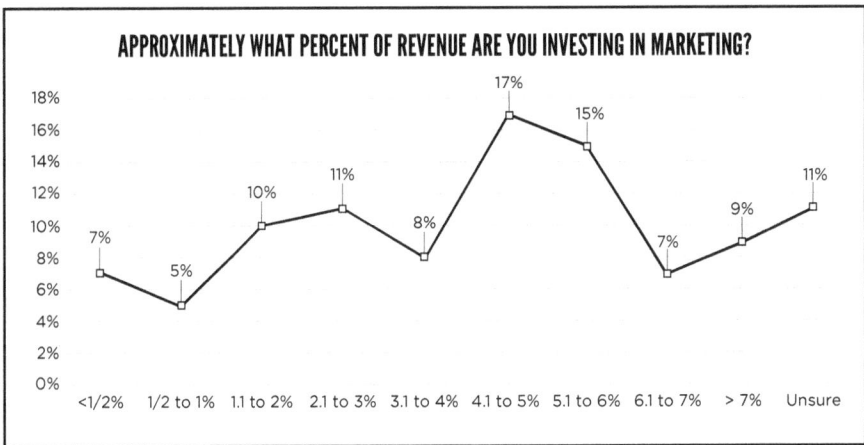

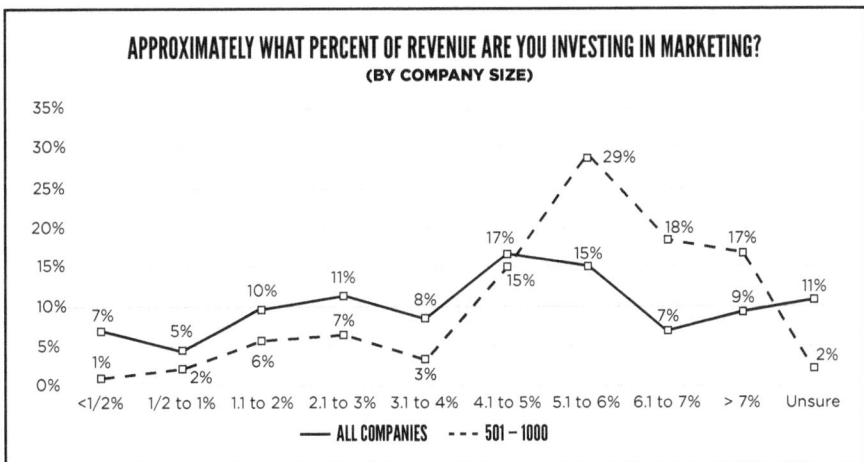

APPROXIMATELY WHAT PERCENT OF REVENUE ARE YOU INVESTING IN MARKETING?

	<1/2%	1/2 to 1%	1.1 to 2%	2.1 to 3%	3.1 to 4%	4.1 to 5%	5.1 to 6%	6.1 to 7%	> 7%	Unsure
	7%	5%	10%	11%	8%	17%	15%	7%	9%	11%

APPROXIMATELY WHAT PERCENT OF REVENUE ARE YOU INVESTING IN MARKETING?
(BY COMPANY SIZE)

	<1/2%	1/2 to 1%	1.1 to 2%	2.1 to 3%	3.1 to 4%	4.1 to 5%	5.1 to 6%	6.1 to 7%	> 7%	Unsure
ALL COMPANIES	7%	5%	10%	11%	8%	17%	15%	7%	9%	11%
501 – 1000	1%	2%	6%	7%	3%	15%	29%	18%	17%	2%

Market Research Investment

Favored marketing research efforts

Respondents were asked to "select all" from a list of the most crucial market research efforts that B2B companies should be executing. Customer or prospect surveys ranked highest with 56 percent of companies executing them. Fifty percent of companies executed industry research. Strikingly, none of the other six market research efforts had even 50 percent of respondents engaging. Most surprising, only 40 percent of respondents had executed a competitive assessment—perhaps the most fundamental and crucial of the research protocols available to B2B leaders. Bottom line: There are miles of opportunity for middle-market B2Bs to improve marketing plan performance if they have sufficient research backing their marketing strategy development.

Over the last three decades in marketing, I've learned that middle-market companies can compete head-to-head for market share against their much larger counterparts if they invest in market research. Market research is the great equalizer. It drives the insights that allow a company to create a scalable, repeatable, and predictable marketing plan with high-growth outcomes.

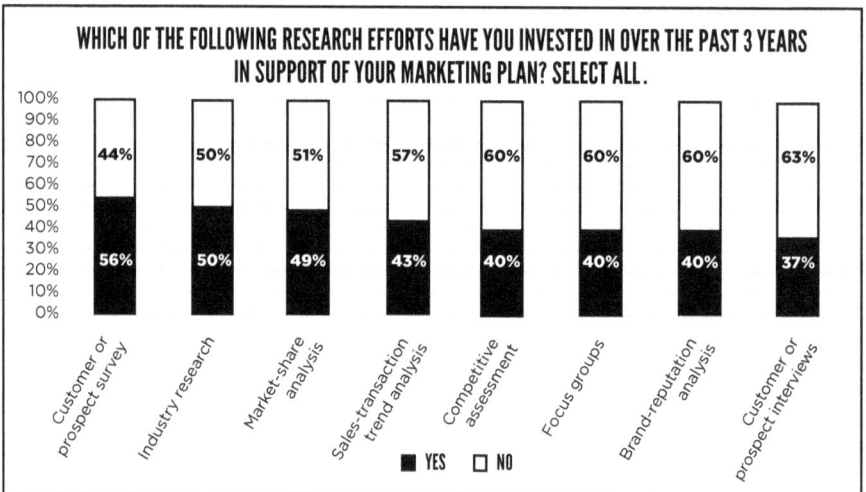

WHICH OF THE FOLLOWING RESEARCH EFFORTS HAVE YOU INVESTED IN OVER THE PAST 3 YEARS IN SUPPORT OF YOUR MARKETING PLAN? SELECT ALL.

Research effort	YES	NO
Customer or prospect survey	56%	44%
Industry research	50%	50%
Market-share analysis	49%	51%
Sales-transaction trend analysis	43%	57%
Competitive assessment	40%	60%
Focus groups	40%	60%
Brand-reputation analysis	40%	60%
Customer or prospect interviews	37%	63%

Why they haven't invested

Of the reasons respondents haven't invested in market research over the past three years, cost tops the list followed by a preference to invest those dollars into marketing execution, which, arguably, is often also a cost concern. More than one third of respondents haven't thought about the need for market research to support their marketing efforts. Forty percent cite not having the internal or external (via an agency partner) expertise as the reason why they lack market research. And 19 percent of survey respondents don't currently see the value in this research. If that's you, my job is to encourage you to battle that thinking and consider an alternative approach, which I'll cover in Battle 3.

WHY HAVEN'T YOU EXECUTED MARKET RESEARCH OVER THE PAST THREE YEARS? SELECT ALL.

Reason	Percent
Too expensive	55%
Would rather use those dollars to invest in marketing	45%
Haven't thought about it	36%
My agency doesn't have the expertise	21%
Don't see the value	19%
Don't have the internal expertise	19%
Unsure	10%
n/a	2%

MROI, CAC, and LTV Benchmarks

MROI

Most respondents report generating a $3:$1 to $4:$1 return on their marketing investment, meaning for every dollar spent, they generate $3 to $4 in return. Eleven percent report not calculating MROI or calculating it but not trusting the data. If you're in that camp, there are significant opportunities for you to improve the performance of your marketing plan—starting with knowing your baseline performance, which will be covered in Battle 4.

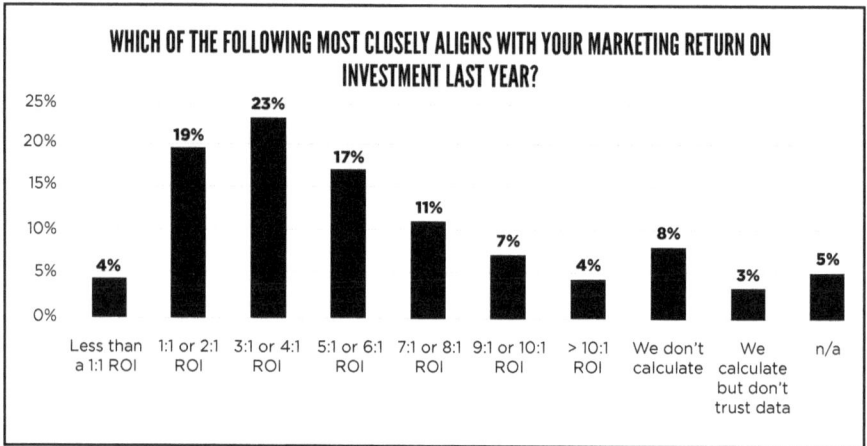

WHICH OF THE FOLLOWING MOST CLOSELY ALIGNS WITH YOUR MARKETING RETURN ON INVESTMENT LAST YEAR?

Less than a 1:1 ROI	4%
1:1 or 2:1 ROI	19%
3:1 or 4:1 ROI	23%
5:1 or 6:1 ROI	17%
7:1 or 8:1 ROI	11%
9:1 or 10:1 ROI	7%
> 10:1 ROI	4%
We don't calculate	8%
We calculate but don't trust data	3%
n/a	5%

When reviewing this MROI data, survey responses make it clear that most companies don't include marketing team compensation in their costs, and most use gross revenue versus gross profit, so these numbers are likely inflated from a purist view of MROI calculations. Also note that these numbers will swing widely by industry. In some industries, a $1.2:$1 MROI is exceptional; in others, a $6:$1 MROI is the industry standard.

Unsurprisingly, larger budgets improve MROI outcomes. Why? A larger budget allows for:

- More frequent exposure of a brand to its target audience.

- More money to invest in creating higher quality content that better engages.

- More money to invest in advanced tools and technologies.

- More money to hire more capable talent.

- More money to engage in greater experimentation with new marketing channels and strategies.

- More money to invest in more comprehensive market research and insights.

CAC and LTV

For middle-market B2Bs, the average CAC is $4,537 with an average customer lifespan of five years and an average transaction size of $59,704. Thus, the average LTV is $298,520 across middle-market B2B respondents. When comparing average CAC, however, note that most respondents fail to include some of the big marketing costs that should always be included, such as marketing agency fees, marketing team compensation, and marketing platform costs. A more conservative CAC calculation, which even fewer companies use, includes both the forgotten marketing expenses just mentioned plus all sales expenses, sales team compensation, and sales platform costs.

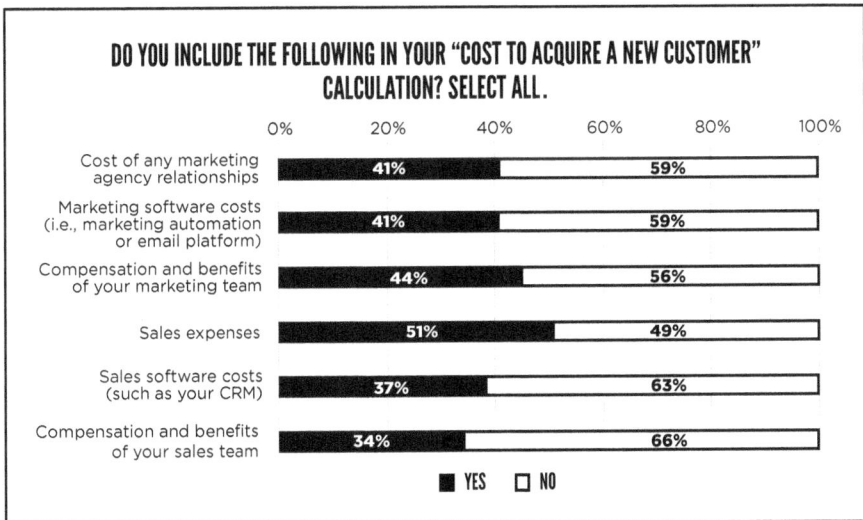

DO YOU INCLUDE THE FOLLOWING IN YOUR "COST TO ACQUIRE A NEW CUSTOMER" CALCULATION? SELECT ALL.

	YES	NO
Cost of any marketing agency relationships	41%	59%
Marketing software costs (i.e., marketing automation or email platform)	41%	59%
Compensation and benefits of your marketing team	44%	56%
Sales expenses	51%	49%
Sales software costs (such as your CRM)	37%	63%
Compensation and benefits of your sales team	34%	66%

In-House Versus Agency Team

Marketing agencies continue to play a pivotal role in supporting the marketing needs of middle-market B2B companies. Nearly 65 percent of respondents use an agency partner to execute all or part of their marketing strategy, with the majority of those (47 percent) leveraging both an agency and an internal team.

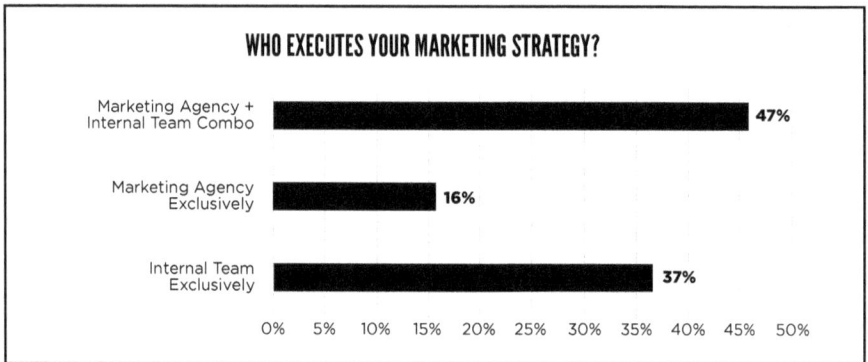

WHO EXECUTES YOUR MARKETING STRATEGY?

Category	Percentage
Marketing Agency + Internal Team Combo	47%
Marketing Agency Exclusively	16%
Internal Team Exclusively	37%

Of those currently using an agency partner, the top two factors that will most influence the choice of their next agency partner are the agency's accountability to its performance and the performance guarantees offered. These are followed by industry expertise, the strategy presented, the reputation of the agency, and the overall ROI of the partnership. Note that projected lead volume landed last on the list, no doubt to the chagrin of the thousands of "pay per lead" shops that have cropped up across the country over the last few years. The data supports the desires of middle-market B2B leaders for accountability deeper than simply lead volume—true accountability and guarantees around new business secured and MROI.

IN SELECTING YOUR NEXT AGENCY PARTNER, WHAT ARE THE TOP THREE FACTORS THAT WILL INFLUENCE YOUR DECISION? SELECT ALL.

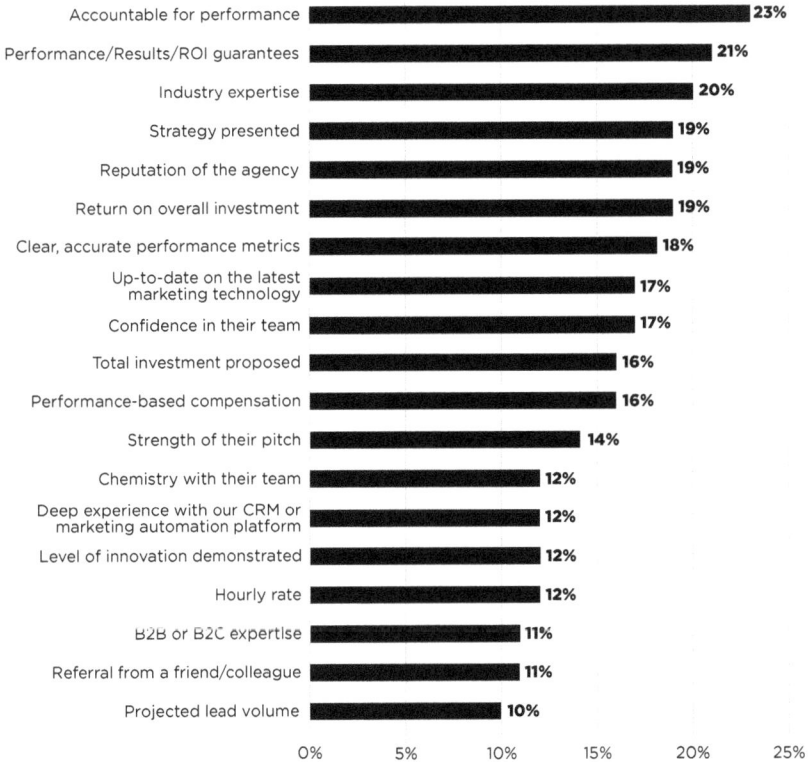

Factor	Percentage
Accountable for performance	23%
Performance/Results/ROI guarantees	21%
Industry expertise	20%
Strategy presented	19%
Reputation of the agency	19%
Return on overall investment	19%
Clear, accurate performance metrics	18%
Up-to-date on the latest marketing technology	17%
Confidence in their team	17%
Total investment proposed	16%
Performance-based compensation	16%
Strength of their pitch	14%
Chemistry with their team	12%
Deep experience with our CRM or marketing automation platform	12%
Level of innovation demonstrated	12%
Hourly rate	12%
B2B or B2C expertise	11%
Referral from a friend/colleague	11%
Projected lead volume	10%

Satisfaction With MROI

Just 24 percent of CEO respondents strongly agree they are highly satisfied with the MROI their current marketing agency provides, which means that 76 percent don't strongly agree. Forty-nine percent of CEO respondents agree with the statement, while 27 percent are neutral or dissatisfied, indicating that there is notable room for improvement and increased expectations. Interestingly, VPs and directors of marketing were generally more optimistic about agency performance.

I AM HIGHLY SATISFIED WITH THE ROI MY CURRENT MARKETING AGENCY PROVIDES.

	Strongly Agree	Agree	Neither Agree Nor Disagree	Disagree	Strongly Disagree
CEO	24%	49%	14%	10%	3%
VP/Director of Marketing	34%	47%	15%	4%	0%

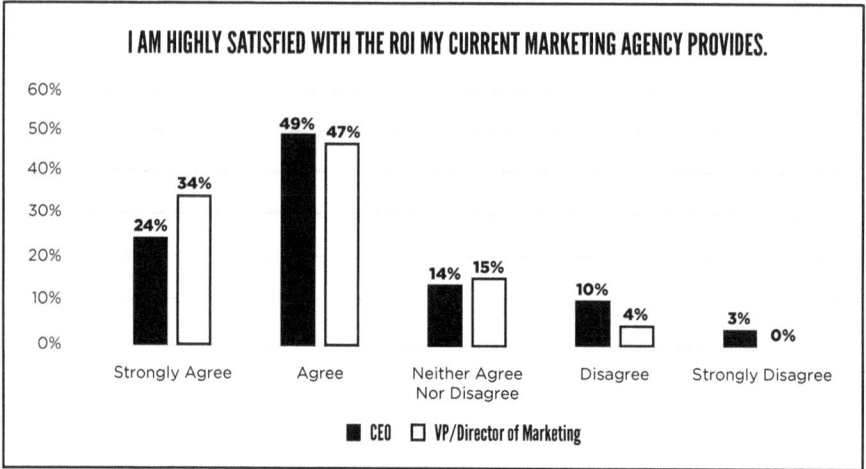

When looking at respondents whose agencies offer a guarantee, the strongly agree scores spike up to 47 percent. Contrast that with only 15 percent of respondents who strongly agree that they are highly satisfied with the MROI provided by their agencies that don't offer a guarantee. B2B leaders are more satisfied with and loyal to agencies that stand behind their growth projections.

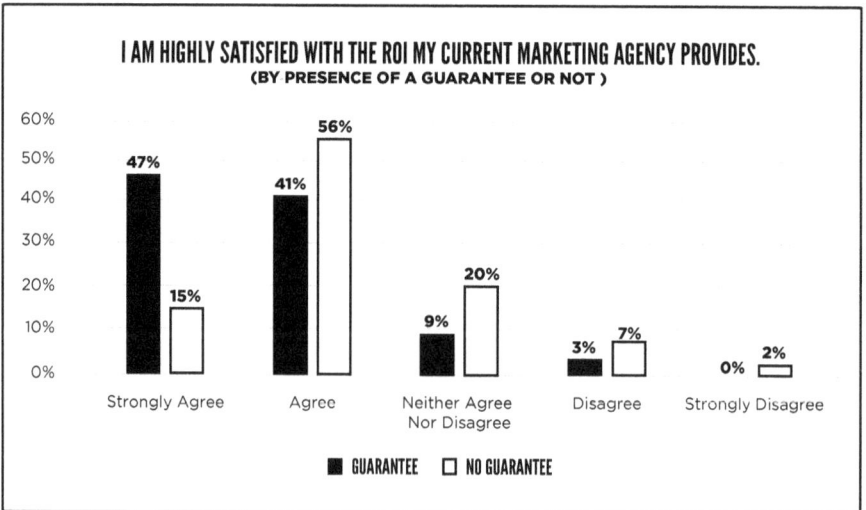

I AM HIGHLY SATISFIED WITH THE ROI MY CURRENT MARKETING AGENCY PROVIDES.
(BY PRESENCE OF A GUARANTEE OR NOT)

	Strongly Agree	Agree	Neither Agree Nor Disagree	Disagree	Strongly Disagree
GUARANTEE	47%	41%	9%	3%	0%
NO GUARANTEE	15%	56%	20%	7%	2%

Guaranteed Marketing Outcomes

Outcomes that are guaranteed

More than half (55 percent) of respondents do not receive any type of agency guarantee. Just 16 percent either pay for each lead received, which is a form of a guarantee, or receive a lead volume guarantee. Another 16 percent get a satisfaction guarantee. And only 14 percent receive an MROI performance guarantee. As referenced in the "In-House Versus Agency Team" section of this survey summary, the top two factors that will most influence a company's future agency partner choice are the agency's accountability to its performance and the performance guarantees offered. The lowest performing factor is projected lead volume, which again supports giving more credence to MROI guarantees.

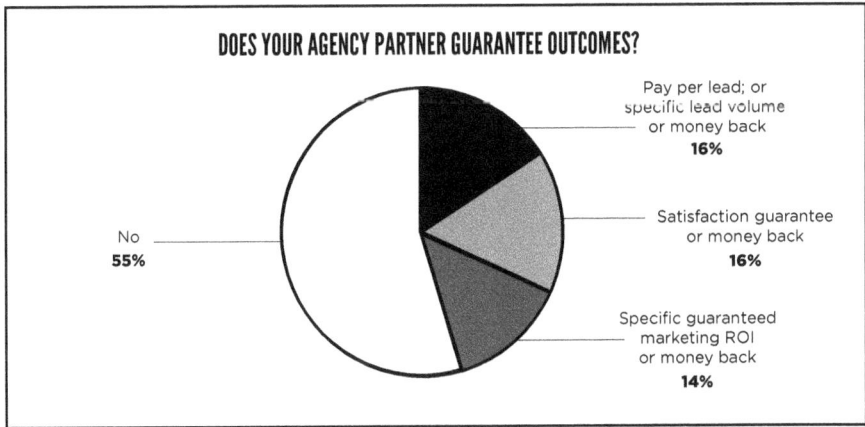

DOES YOUR AGENCY PARTNER GUARANTEE OUTCOMES?

Pay per lead; or specific lead volume or money back **16%**

Satisfaction guarantee or money back **16%**

Specific guaranteed marketing ROI or money back **14%**

No **55%**

The "impossibility" of predicting outcomes

Most respondents believe that their marketing teams can't accurately predict outcomes because the market is too competitive, the team needs more time, or there is not enough research to inform the strategy. The last of these factors is supported by the fact that fewer than half of respondents have executed most of the common market research practices that are considered must-haves to inform a predictable marketing plan.

More than twice the number of respondents cite the degree of market competition as the reason for lack of marketing predictability (32 percent) as compared to those who believe they don't have the right strategy (14 percent). Could it be possible that the market wouldn't be as competitive with the right research-backed strategy?

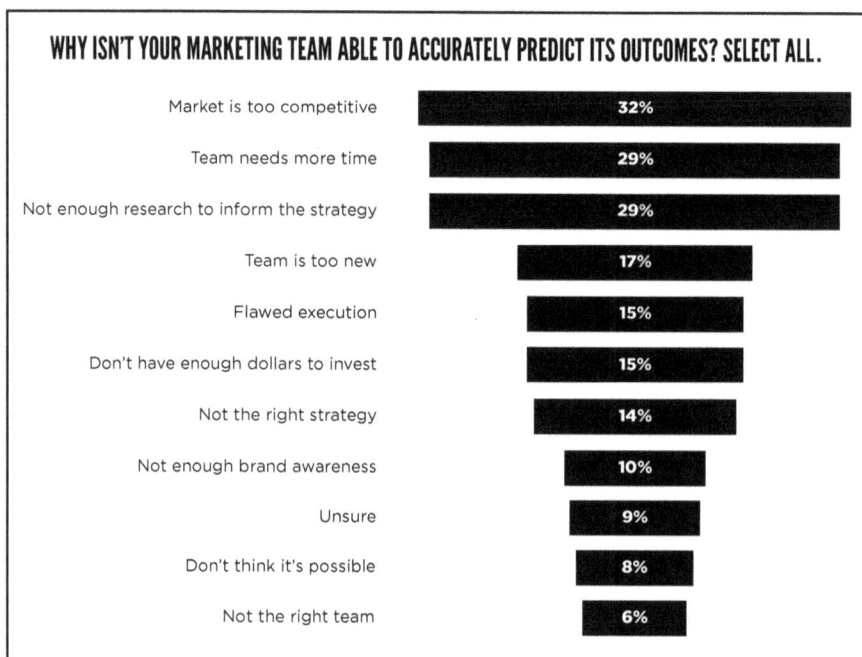

WHY ISN'T YOUR MARKETING TEAM ABLE TO ACCURATELY PREDICT ITS OUTCOMES? SELECT ALL.

Category	Percent
Market is too competitive	32%
Team needs more time	29%
Not enough research to inform the strategy	29%
Team is too new	17%
Flawed execution	15%
Don't have enough dollars to invest	15%
Not the right strategy	14%
Not enough brand awareness	10%
Unsure	9%
Don't think it's possible	8%
Not the right team	6%

Why there are so few guarantees

When respondents were asked why they believe most agencies don't offer a results guarantee, the number one answer was that it's "too risky for the agency." This was followed by it's "impossible to predict marketing outcomes" and it's "too complicated to determine lead source." Are any of these really true? Or are these myths propagated by an industry that's scared to raise the bar and stand behind its performance?

WHY DO YOU BELIEVE MOST AGENCIES DON'T OFFER A RESULTS GUARANTEE?

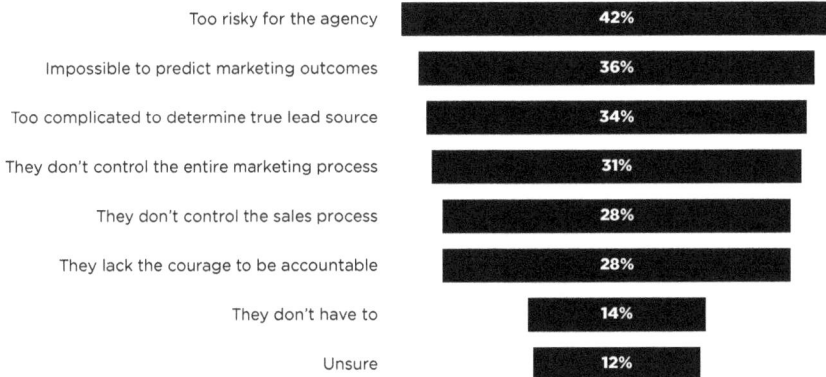

Too risky for the agency	42%
Impossible to predict marketing outcomes	36%
Too complicated to determine true lead source	34%
They don't control the entire marketing process	31%
They don't control the sales process	28%
They lack the courage to be accountable	28%
They don't have to	14%
Unsure	12%

Tellingly, when asked if they would be more likely to partner with an agency that offers a guaranteed return on their marketing investment, 83 percent of respondents either agreed or strongly agreed.

I WOULD BE MORE LIKELY TO PARTNER WITH AN AGENCY THAT OFFERS A GUARANTEED RETURN ON MY OVERALL MARKETING INVESTMENT.

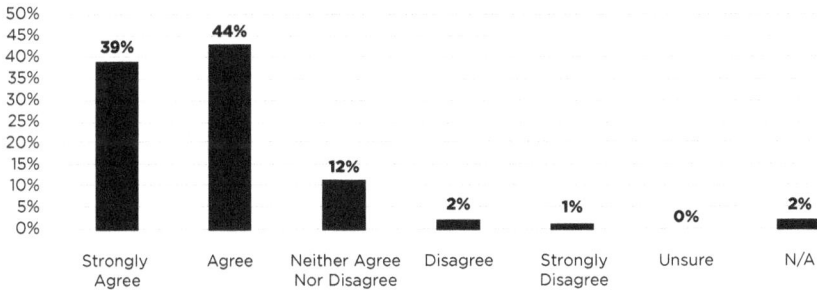

Strongly Agree	Agree	Neither Agree Nor Disagree	Disagree	Strongly Disagree	Unsure	N/A
39%	44%	12%	2%	1%	0%	2%

The top two factors that most influence respondents' likelihood to partner with a marketing agency that offers a guaranteed return on investment are "the confidence I would have in an agency willing to take accountability and stand behind its projections" and "the ability to focus on other areas of the company's operations, knowing my marketing agency has true accountability for performance."

WHAT MOST INFLUENCES YOUR LIKELIHOOD TO PARTNER WITH AN AGENCY OFFERING A GUARANTEED RETURN ON INVESTMENT?

Factor	Percentage
The confidence I would have in an agency willing to take accountability and stand behind its projections	45%
The ability to focus on other areas of the company's operations, knowing my marketing agency has true accountability for performance	45%
The ability to better predict growth	30%
The freedom of not having to worry about the performance of my marketing plan	28%
The ability to derisk my marketing investment	18%

Scalable, Repeatable, and Predictable Marketing Plans

Respondents were asked if their marketing plan is scalable, with scalable defined as the ability to maintain at or above the current level of marketing performance as marketing investment increases. In other words, if they were to pour fuel on their existing strategy, would it still perform as well at the higher investment level? Twenty-four percent indicated they strongly agreed with the statement while 50 percent agreed. More than a quarter were neutral, disagreed, or were unsure. A company's ability to scale its marketing efforts is critical to predictable growth.

MY CURRENT MARKETING PLAN IS SCALABLE.

Response	Percentage
Strongly Agree	24%
Agree	50%
Neither Agree Nor Disagree	19%
Disagree	4%
Strongly Disagree	0%
Unsure	3%

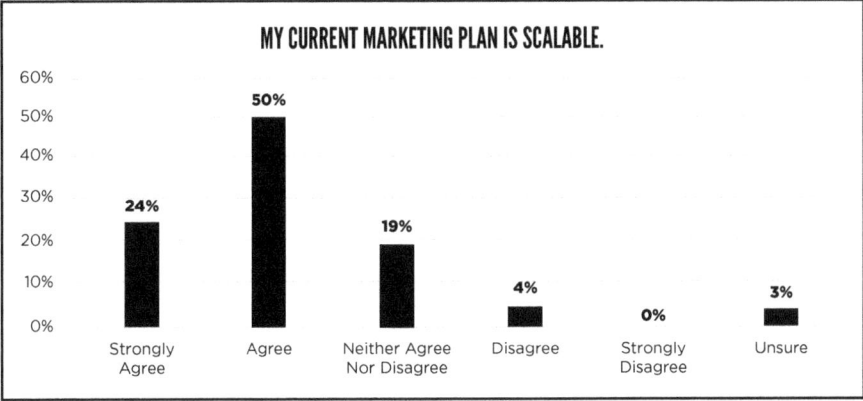

Similarly, respondents were asked if their marketing plan is repeatable, with repeatable defined as the ability to maintain current marketing performance, usually due in large part to documented processes, no matter who on the team is executing the strategy in the future. Twenty-eight percent indicated they strongly agreed with the statement while 50 percent agreed. More than 20 percent were neutral, disagreed, or were unsure. Companies with a repeatable marketing strategy see consistent performance despite key employee turnover—a necessary component to a scalable marketing plan.

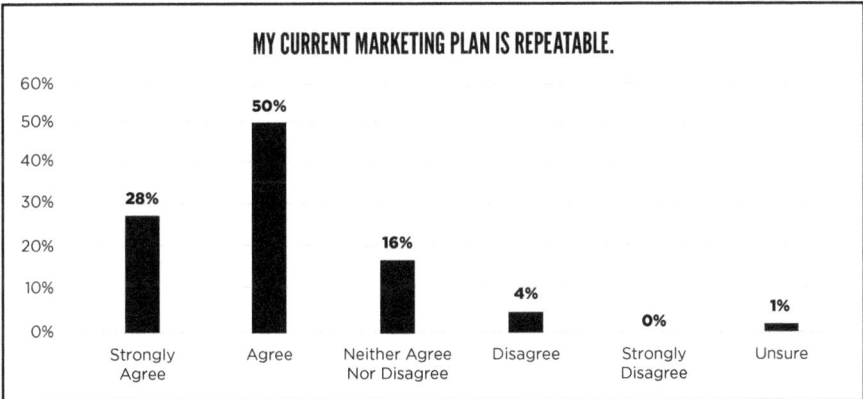

MY CURRENT MARKETING PLAN IS REPEATABLE.

Response	Percentage
Strongly Agree	28%
Agree	50%
Neither Agree Nor Disagree	16%
Disagree	4%
Strongly Disagree	0%
Unsure	1%

Respondents were also asked if their marketing plan is predictable, with predictable defined as the ability to project the new business growth that will be generated by executing an established marketing strategy(ies). Twenty-one percent indicated they strongly agreed with the statement while 47 percent agreed. Thirty-two percent were neutral, disagreed, or were unsure. Predictability is the holy grail of marketing and certainly a requirement for guaranteed outcomes. Predictability allows the operations team to scale up in a planned and intentional way, which reduces friction in the customer experience and, therefore, customer churn. The 12 Battles™ Framework is specifically designed to infuse this scalability, repeatability, and predictability into your marketing plan.

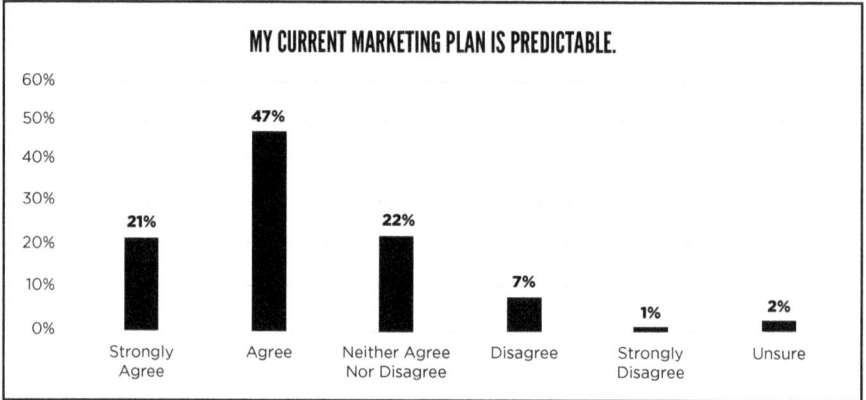

MY CURRENT MARKETING PLAN IS PREDICTABLE.

Category	Percentage
Strongly Agree	21%
Agree	47%
Neither Agree Nor Disagree	22%
Disagree	7%
Strongly Disagree	1%
Unsure	2%

One way to make your marketing strategies scalable, repeatable, and predictable is regular campaign optimization. The best practice is weekly optimization; only 7 percent of respondents execute at this frequency.

HOW FREQUENTLY DOES YOUR TEAM OPTIMIZE YOUR MARKETING STRATEGIES?

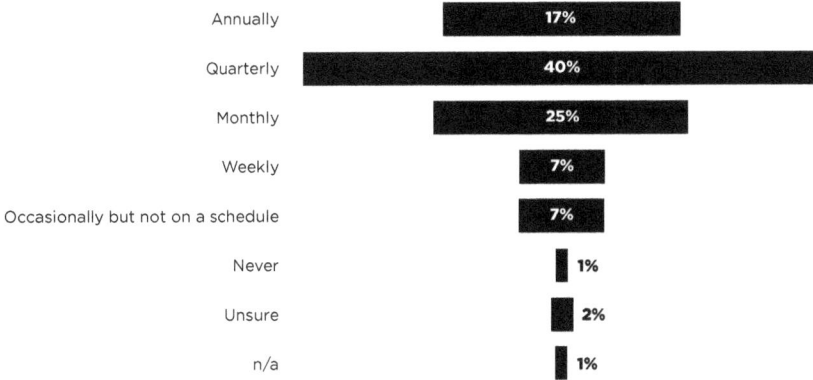

Annually	17%
Quarterly	40%
Monthly	25%
Weekly	7%
Occasionally but not on a schedule	7%
Never	1%
Unsure	2%
n/a	1%

Performance-Based Compensation

The majority of respondents confirmed that, to at least some degree, their team's total compensation—whether it be an internal or external team—is tied to company performance, though only 18 percent were in the strongly agree camp. It's notable that performance-based compensation is more prevalent among respondents with agency teams than it is among those with internal teams only. This reveals an opportunity to level up internal compensation plans to better align with marketing performance and growth goals.

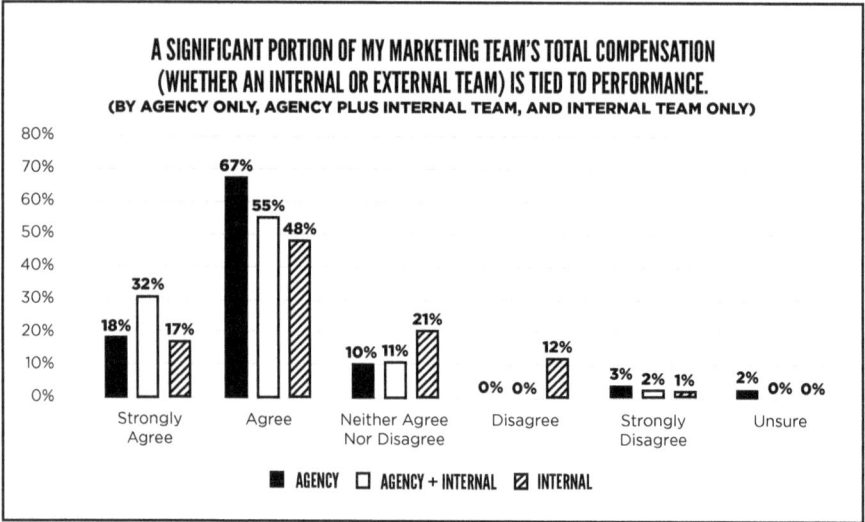

A SIGNIFICANT PORTION OF MY MARKETING TEAM'S TOTAL COMPENSATION (WHETHER AN INTERNAL OR EXTERNAL TEAM) IS TIED TO PERFORMANCE.
(BY AGENCY ONLY, AGENCY PLUS INTERNAL TEAM, AND INTERNAL TEAM ONLY)

	Strongly Agree	Agree	Neither Agree Nor Disagree	Disagree	Strongly Disagree	Unsure
AGENCY	18%	67%	10%	0%	3%	2%
AGENCY + INTERNAL	32%	55%	11%	0%	2%	0%
INTERNAL	17%	48%	21%	12%	1%	0%

Conclusion

As the foundation for *The B2B Marketing Revolution*™, this study clearly shows that a significant majority of middle-market companies are channeling a notable portion of their revenue into marketing, recognizing its vital role in amplifying their growth. Yet, alongside this investment, there's a palpable uncertainty—about how to generate stronger plan performance, whether to tie team compensation to performance and to what degree, and about how to craft marketing plans that are truly scalable, repeatable, and predictable. There is also apprehension toward market research, which is often dismissed as too costly—a hesitation driven by cost misconceptions that ignore the greater risk of navigating without insights.

Despite general contentment with MROI, there's an underlying desire for more—more reliability, more precision, and more strategic clarity. There is a clear preference among middle-market B2B leaders for agency partners with skin in the game, those willing to stand behind their performance projections and offer guarantees.

This is the beginning of a revolution in B2B marketing—where clients forcibly raise the bar on an industry that is reluctant to do so itself.

12 BATTLES™ FRAMEWORK

1. YOU **ACCEPT** THAT YOU DESERVE AND WILL ACHIEVE GUARANTEED MARKETING OUTCOMES.

2. YOU **ACKNOWLEDGE** THAT YOU DON'T REALLY KNOW THY CUSTOMER.

3. YOU **CHAMPION** MARKET RESEARCH AS A DO-OR-DIE INVESTMENT.

4. YOU **EMBRACE** THE POWER OF ATTRIBUTION MODELING AND STOP ACCEPTING BAD DATA.

5. YOU **OWN** AN OPENING IN THE BRANDSCAPE.

6. YOU **TORCH** YOUR EXISTING STRATEGY UNAPOLOGETICALLY IF NEEDED.

7. YOU **ADVOCATE** FOR AN INVESTMENT IN EACH STAGE OF THE CUSTOMER JOURNEY.

8. YOU **CHALLENGE** YOUR TEAM TO MAKE POWERFUL STRATEGIC SHIFTS GROUNDED IN RESEARCH VERSUS TRADITION.

9. YOU **PREACH** THE GOOD WORD OF DISCIPLINED OPTIMIZATION.

10. YOU **COMMIT** TO BUILDING A PAY-FOR-PERFORMANCE TEAM AROUND YOUR STRATEGY; NOT VICE VERSA.

11. YOU **REQUIRE** A POWERFUL MARKETING DASHBOARD AND DOCUMENTED PROCESSES.

12. YOU **INSPIRE** YOUR TEAM TO STAND BEHIND THEIR MROI PROJECTIONS.

BATTLE 1 : YOU **ACCEPT** THAT YOU DESERVE AND WILL ACHIEVE GUARANTEED MARKETING OUTCOMES

Battle 1

Battle 1 asks you to do something radical. It asks you to believe you deserve it. It asks you to believe you will achieve your desired marketing results. It asks you to believe that success can be guaranteed. It's about defying the apathy the industry expects of you and declaring, "I deserve guaranteed marketing outcomes, and anyone standing in my way will be lovingly removed."

Maybe you're asking yourself what a results-guaranteed marketing strategy is? Refined down to its purest form, a results-guaranteed marketing strategy is how you expand while everyone else is contracting. It's how you shift from growing by accident to growing with intent and on purpose. It's how you create predictable performance that drives up company valuation for a transaction or investment pitch. It's how you know how aggressively you should plan to scale operations. The bottom line: It's how you build your legacy.

A results-guaranteed marketing strategy goes beyond the typical S.M.A.R.T. plan—beyond specific, measurable, achievable, relevant, and time bound. It's about creating a predictable plan that instills 100 percent confidence and that your internal or external marketing teams have the courage and conviction to stand behind.

The concept of guaranteed marketing outcomes is a premise that challenges the very foundation of conventional thinking because marketing is both an art and a science. The two most common questions I get asked are some variation of: "How can I predict the performance of something as subjective as marketing," and "How can I predict something as fickle as consumer behavior?" The answer to both is that you can predict future customer behavior within a reasonable margin of error based on their past behavior and what they've disclosed about their future intentions—all of which can be uncovered through targeted market research.

When I sat in your shoes, on the client side of the table, I heard every excuse in the book about why the agencies I hired couldn't stand behind their projected outcomes. At its core, the essence of why is that the traditional marketing agency model has become obsolete. Let's leave behind the days when paying for pretty but ineffective campaigns or for an agency's time versus their performance was acceptable. You must stop settling for agencies that don't have enough conviction in their own projections to have skin in the game. If an agency isn't willing to offer a guarantee on their projections, walk away. The same goes for your internal team once they're armed with the 12 Battles™ Framework.

> **THE REAL REASON AGENCIES DON'T STAND BEHIND THEIR PROJECTIONS IS THAT THE TRADITIONAL MARKETING AGENCY MODEL IS OBSOLETE.**

Yes, marketing *is* both art and science; the market *is* dynamic; an agency or internal team *can't* measure everything; and marketers usually *can't* control 100 percent of your conversion process. All these things are true, and they are common mantras from traditional agency leaders. But, at the end of the day, as marketers, if we aren't willing to stand behind our own projected outcomes, why the hell are we in this business? You deserve better.

> **IF WE AREN'T WILLING TO STAND BEHIND OUR OWN PROJECTED OUTCOMES, WHY THE HELL ARE WE IN THIS BUSINESS?**

Skepticism

There are three primary reasons why marketers often are skeptical that marketing results can be predicted and even guaranteed.

Reason 1: Fear of Raising the Bar
The first and perhaps most profound reason for the skepticism is fear of raising the bar. The thought of significantly elevating expectations can be downright terrifying, and rightfully so. Why risk putting a stake in the ground and back up your projections with a guarantee when the conventional approach is considered good enough?

Fear of raising the bar often stems from a fear of moving out of your comfort zone, which has worked for so long that raising the bar comes with the risk of failure. You must recognize that true progress often lies beyond the boundaries of comfort. Revolutionary change rarely occurs when you cling to the familiar. To achieve guaranteed marketing outcomes, you must get comfortable being uncomfortable.

Reason 2: Absence of Properly Structured Teams
The second reason behind the skepticism is the absence of teams properly structured to deliver predictable, guaranteed outcomes. What

does a team that is built for guaranteed outcomes look like? It's a team that approaches marketing with a results-oriented mindset from the ground up.

A results-oriented team is one that:

- **Hires, fires, rewards, and promotes based on outcomes:** Every team member's performance is tied to their ability to drive outcomes. Those who consistently deliver results are rewarded, and those who don't are held accountable.

- **Measures outcomes regularly:** Outcomes are measured not as an afterthought but as a routine part of operations. Weekly assessments are conducted, and outcomes are transparently shared across the organization.

- **Values client outcomes:** Core values are structured around outcomes. Measurable success becomes a guiding principle that permeates company culture.

- **Emphasizes training:** Comprehensive training and coaching programs are in place within the organization to develop the skills and knowledge needed to consistently achieve outcomes. This industry is wildly dynamic. If you aren't sharpening your skills every quarter at a minimum, you're obsolete.

- **Follows documented processes:** The team relies on written processes that have proven effective in driving consistent marketing outcomes.

- **Displays leadership and accountability:** Leadership is marked by the courage to plant a flag and take accountability for projections and outcomes.

Creating a results-oriented team upsets the norm. It requires a shift in mindset, an adjustment in how success is defined, and often a restructure to ensure that outcomes are prioritized. For example, at RedRover, we are structured into three divisions—Client Outcomes, Client Strategy, and Client Experience. Having specific, focused leadership over Client Outcomes ensures clear accountability for achievement of projected metrics.

Reason 3: Lack of Market Research Chops

The third reason behind the skepticism of guaranteed marketing outcomes is the lack of a market research team with deep qualitative and quantitative capabilities. In its simplest terms, qualitative research is where you explore perspectives and opinions, and quantitative research is where you explore data. Both are essential to a results-guaranteed marketing plan. Effective marketing strategies are built on a foundation of market insights and an extensive understanding of customer behavior. Without these insights, the most creative and engaging campaigns will still fall short.

A market research expert or team with qualitative and quantitative chops is crucial for:

- **Uncovering unknown openings in the market:** Deep market research can reveal unknown marketplace opportunities—sometimes massive openings in the market for you to steal market share. The objectivity that a market research professional brings to the table is essential for game-changing discoveries.

- **Identifying hidden optimization opportunities:** Leveraging an objective third-party market research expert often results in their identifying otherwise hidden opportunities for marketing plan optimizations that you are simply too close to see.

- **Seeing new customer data trends:** A market research expert will often see trends in your customer data that can make or break your marketing strategy—trends that your passion and knowledge for your company may not easily allow you to see. For example, you likely don't have full transparency into why lost customers left your company. They generally only share what they want you to know. You probably also don't have complete clarity into all the reasons why a customer chooses your competitor over you in a head-to-head matchup and how they rank order those decision-making criteria.

- **Formulating a backbone for your guarantee:** Market research provides the necessary insights to make informed projections—critical insights such as what messaging and offer strategies will sway customers to buy more from you, how much they're open to buying, and how your marketing plan will perform against competitor marketing. The bottom line: You can't calculate accurate projections without quality research.

In an industry filled with small agencies, more than 90 percent lack the highly specialized market research skills required for such predictability. It's imperative you find a marketing agency with deep research chops or a dedicated marketing research shop that can bring objectivity to your research efforts.

CHECK OUT THE 12 BATTLES™ READER HUB at marketingtoolsforyou.com for this free resource:

AGENCY "LEVELING UP" SCRIPT

The most common reason so few middle-market companies excel in creating predictable, high-performance marketing plans is that they don't know how to get there. While the path isn't simple, it's proven. The comprehensive 12 Battles™ Framework, when followed diligently, can transform an underperforming, unpredictable, and non-scalable marketing strategy from a cost center to a revenue generator.

Overthrowing the Status Quo

Learning how to embrace change is a fundamental aspect of the journey toward guaranteed marketing outcomes, and there's no one better to lead the way than you. I encourage you to challenge established norms and question traditional approaches to marketing. To truly embrace change, you—as a marketing leader or CEO—must be willing to:

- **Challenge the comfort zone:** It's instinctive to stick to what's familiar and comfortable. However, achieving guaranteed outcomes often requires stepping outside of this comfort zone. It means acknowledging that the familiar may not always be the most effective approach.

- **Redefine success:** Traditional success metrics will no longer suffice. Instead of measuring success solely by the number of leads or clicks generated, consider a more comprehensive view, such as the gross profit your company generates from new customers and their likely lifetime value.

- **Foster a culture of innovation:** Revolution thrives in environments that encourage innovation. Encourage your team to explore new ideas, experiment with different strategies, and be open to calculated risks.

Fear often accompanies the concept of guarantees in marketing. It's the fear of commitment, the fear of falling short, and the fear of accountability. However, this fear can be a powerful motivator for excellence. To overcome the fear of guarantees, be sure to:

- **Set realistic expectations:** Guarantees don't mean promising the impossible. They mean committing to achievable, data-backed outcomes.

- **Leverage fear as motivation:** Rather than letting fear paralyze your team, use it as a source of motivation. The fear of failing to meet guarantees can drive your team to push boundaries and deliver exceptional results.

- **Build trust through transparency and communication:** Build trust by maintaining transparency with your internal team. Communicate your commitment to generating guaranteed marketing outcomes, explain the 12 Battles™ Framework used to arrive at those predictable targets, and outline the support you're willing to put behind the effort.

What follows in this book is a deep dive into the 12 Battles™ Framework using real-life examples of both successes and cautionary tales, as well as actionable steps to guide you through your marketing revolution. They are not standalone concepts but interconnected elements of a holistic approach to marketing excellence. Embracing and implementing these elements within your organization will pave the way for guaranteed marketing outcomes. Are you ready to start a revolution?

Battle 1 Research Insights[2]

24% of middle-market B2B CEOs are highly satisfied with the MROI their current marketing agency provides, indicating room for improvement.

---

[2] From the "2024 RedRover U.S. Middle-Market B2B Marketing Performance Study," available in the 12 Battles™ Reader Hub at marketingtoolsforyou.com.

55% of marketing agencies do not offer a performance guarantee, yet 83 percent of respondents agree or strongly agree they are more likely to partner with an agency that offers a guaranteed return on their overall marketing investment. What most influences their likelihood to partner with an agency that offers guaranteed MROI are: "the confidence I would have in an agency willing to take accountability and stand behind its projections" and "the ability to focus on other areas of the company's operations."

42% of respondents believe that most agencies don't offer a guarantee because it's "too risky for the agency." Thirty-six percent say it's "impossible to predict marketing outcomes." I believe this is what traditional agencies tell their clients both because they are understandably nervous about leveling up their accountability since they don't have the framework or structure to do so and because clients don't yet demand it.

32% of respondents say their marketing team isn't able to accurately predict its outcomes due to the market being too competitive. Twenty-nine percent say it's due to not having enough research to inform the strategy. I often find that the market wouldn't be as competitive with the right research-backed strategy.

START A REVOLUTION: ACCEPT THAT YOU DESERVE AND WILL ACHIEVE GUARANTEED MARKETING OUTCOMES.

---

12 BATTLES™ FRAMEWORK

1 — YOU **ACCEPT** THAT YOU DESERVE AND WILL ACHIEVE GUARANTEED MARKETING OUTCOMES.

2 — YOU **ACKNOWLEDGE** THAT YOU DON'T REALLY KNOW THY CUSTOMER.

3 — YOU **CHAMPION** MARKET RESEARCH AS A DO-OR-DIE INVESTMENT.

4 — YOU **EMBRACE** THE POWER OF ATTRIBUTION MODELING AND STOP ACCEPTING BAD DATA.

5 — YOU **OWN** AN OPENING IN THE BRANDSCAPE.

6 — YOU **TORCH** YOUR EXISTING STRATEGY UNAPOLOGETICALLY IF NEEDED.

7 — YOU **ADVOCATE** FOR AN INVESTMENT IN EACH STAGE OF THE CUSTOMER JOURNEY.

8 — YOU **CHALLENGE** YOUR TEAM TO MAKE POWERFUL STRATEGIC SHIFTS GROUNDED IN RESEARCH VERSUS TRADITION.

9 — YOU **PREACH** THE GOOD WORD OF DISCIPLINED OPTIMIZATION.

10 — YOU **COMMIT** TO BUILDING A PAY-FOR-PERFORMANCE TEAM AROUND YOUR STRATEGY; NOT VICE VERSA.

11 — YOU **REQUIRE** A POWERFUL MARKETING DASHBOARD AND DOCUMENTED PROCESSES.

12 — YOU **INSPIRE** YOUR TEAM TO STAND BEHIND THEIR MROI PROJECTIONS.

BATTLE 2 : YOU **ACKNOWLEDGE** THAT YOU DON'T REALLY KNOW THY CUSTOMER

Battle 2

Battle 2 compels you to acknowledge that you don't really know thy customer.

Acknowledging that you don't really know your customer is not only a revolution in mindset but a vital one—and perhaps the most challenging to accept. Accepting this premise is the linchpin of your ability to lead a team that creates an effective marketing strategy that drives specific, guaranteed outcomes.

Embracing this truth is a journey that every CEO and marketing leader with tenure must take. You believe on some level that you know more about your customers than anyone externally possibly could because you live, eat, and breathe your business. I've been there. But the truth is you can't possibly know everything you need to know because you are far too close to your business. You are wonderfully biased and subjective. You can't possibly see all of the friction in your sales process or the lack of alignment between your sales and marketing messaging when you have been instrumental in putting them together. You likely struggle to appreciate why a customer would choose your competition because you love your company. From a research perspective, that's the kiss of death. Here your passion doesn't help. You need objectivity—miles of objectivity—and your results-guaranteed marketing strategy is banking on that objectivity.

> **YOU ARE WONDERFULLY BIASED AND SUBJECTIVE. FROM A RESEARCH PERSPECTIVE, THAT'S THE KISS OF DEATH. HERE YOUR PASSION DOESN'T HELP.**

So what should you know about your customers? Following are 10 insights every CEO and marketing leader should know about their customers:

1. **Their motivations, desires, and emotional triggers:** True understanding goes beyond demographics, encompassing psychographics, such as attitudes, values, fears, motivations, and desires. You must dive into the emotional triggers that drive your customers' decisions. For instance, consider the emotional trigger of FOMO (fear of missing out), where customers are driven by the fear of missing exclusive offers and experiences or limited-time opportunities. Alternatively, think about the emotional trigger of exclusivity, where customers are drawn to products or services that make them feel like part of an exclusive club. And don't forget the emotional trigger of belonging and community, where customers are motivated by the desire to connect with like-minded individuals who share their values and interests. These emotional triggers can guide your marketing strategy and help you create meaningful connections with your audience.

2. **Why lost customers really chose to part ways:** Customers who've left can provide critical feedback for improvement—and

often the reason they initially provide just scratches the surface. Understand the actual root cause of why they chose to part ways, and use this information to refine your offerings and delivery. The most effective strategy for uncovering this information is to use a third-party research firm, as your lost customers are more likely to open up to an objective observer who commits to maintaining their confidentiality.

3. **What's stopping prospective customers from becoming loyal customers:** Understanding customer barriers is key to converting leads. Imagine a scenario where prospective customers hesitate due to uncertainty about a product's quality or effectiveness. Addressing this barrier can involve providing transparent product reviews, case studies, or even free trials to build trust and confidence. Additionally, consider situations where price sensitivity is a significant barrier. Offering discounts, bundling options, or flexible payment plans can help overcome this obstacle. Some potential customers might be concerned about the complexity of using your product or service. Providing easy-to-follow tutorials, user-friendly interfaces, and exceptional customer support can remove this barrier, making the conversion process smoother. By identifying and addressing these customer barriers, you can significantly enhance your lead conversion rate.

4. **Why customers choose you over competitors:** Analyze the unique value propositions that set you apart. Understand competitors' strengths, weaknesses, and any gaps that exist in the market. Identify opportunities to outperform rivals and seize market share. All of this can be uncovered through current, lost, and prospective customer interviews and surveys.

5. **How much market share you really have:** What are your customers really spending with you versus competitors and why? A well-crafted customer and prospect survey can provide you with this transparency.

6. **Current customer pain points:** What are they hiding from you so as not to make waves? Here again, your current and lost customer interviews and surveys can be leveraged to uncover these insights.

7. **Customer segmentation opportunities:** The more effectively you segment your target market, the more effectively you can personalize messaging to them. Market research allows you to pinpoint these customer segmentation nuances that could make all the difference in the return on your marketing investment. It allows you to create detailed customer profiles to target your messaging accurately.

8. **Evolving needs:** Customer needs change over time, and staying informed is crucial. You must regularly monitor customer preferences and adapt your offerings accordingly. While a large-scale customer survey may only be needed every five years, a short version could be sent out quarterly.

9. **The customer journey:** What is the typical journey of a prospective customer who lands at your door? What does every typical touchpoint look like along the way? Your prospect's typical journey could look like this: They first meet your team at a trade show where they begin following your brand on social media. Then they visit your website where they download an ebook and sign up for a free webinar. Then they check your online reviews. They conclude by booking a call with the sales team. Once you've identified the typical prospect journey, ask yourself if they are getting the information they want when, how, and where they want it. Are they feeling friction in the process? Are you losing customers at one particular stop along the way?

10. **What they really think about your positioning:** What you may think is an important point of differentiation may not matter

much to your customers. Find out what factors they rank as the most crucial to their buying decision and how an adjustment to your messaging could really break through.

CHECK OUT THE 12 BATTLES™ READER HUB at marketingtoolsforyou.com for this free resource:

SURVEY QUESTIONS FOR 10 CUSTOMER INSIGHTS

The bottom line: It's vital to acknowledge the limitations of your customer knowledge. While you may genuinely believe you know your customers inside and out, the reality is often far more complex. Understanding your customer requires objectivity, which starts with an awareness of the biases that can cloud your judgment.

By embracing the assistance of an external market research specialist or firm, you gain a more comprehensive and objective view of your customer base. These firms offer valuable insights into customer behaviors, motivations, and market dynamics that you may have overlooked. They provide the objectivity needed so that you can make informed strategic decisions and execute marketing initiatives that yield guaranteed outcomes.

CHECK OUT THE 12 BATTLES™ READER HUB at marketingtoolsforyou.com for this free resource:

MARKET RESEARCH FIRM VETTING GUIDE

Battle 2 Research Insights[3]

35% of survey respondents strongly agree that their marketing team knows their targeted customer, including their demographics, behaviors, motivations, preferences, and needs, which leaves miles of opportunity to leverage this linchpin to a fully-optimized, high-performing, and predictable marketing plan.

56% is the maximum participation level by survey respondents over the last three years in any of the fundamental market research best practices that are vital to generating consistent, predictable marketing outcomes. Without this research, no company truly knows its customers and competitors to the degree necessary to fully optimize a marketing plan and drive optimum performance.

Success Story

Star Manufacturing[4], a $20M company in the industrial manufacturing sector, experienced a plateau in growth despite numerous advertising agency partnerships over five years. The vice president of sales and marketing, Hank, sought a new marketing partner who shared his results-driven approach. When Hank engaged my team, he expressed a desire for change and was open to unorthodox strategies.

Our initial discussions centered on aligning our objectives with Hank's key performance indicator: growth in gross profit, as this is what he was bonused on quarterly. Growth in gross profit thus became our goal as well. This client believed, before seeing it come to fruition, that he

---

[3] From the "2024 RedRover U.S. Middle-Market B2B Marketing Performance Study," available in the 12 Battles™ Reader Hub at marketingtoolsforyou.com.
[4] Client details have been modified to respect confidentiality.

deserved and could get a guaranteed MROI. And he was curious to learn everything he could about his targeted customer to strengthen his marketing outreach.

After conducting thorough market research, we uncovered several concerns: Star Manufacturing had a stale brand identity with differentiation that wasn't breaking through; a disorganized CRM (customer relationship management) platform that was obstructing sales and marketing alignment; gaps in its email marketing causing lost leads; a website not optimized for conversions; too much customer concentration in one industry vertical; and inefficiencies in its Google Ads strategy. We also identified what would make its current and past customers spend more with the brand over the competition.

Armed with this data, RedRover developed a 12-month marketing strategy with clear MROI targets that we committed to meeting each quarter. Over a five-year partnership with Hank's team, our efforts led to an overall $2000 return for every $1 invested in marketing, significantly contributing to the company's value at the point of its sale to an international firm. While this exceptional MROI was specific to Star Manufacturing's unique context, it underscores the effectiveness of a data-driven, performance-focused marketing approach.

Hank's endorsement of our results was clear when he advised the acquiring company to uphold the marketing standards RedRover had set as a testament to the sustainable growth and profitability we had helped achieve.

Cautionary Tale

AI-Lift[5], a $10M B2B manufacturer of high-tech forklifts, requested a meeting to explore the role that marketing could play in its future

---

[5] Client details have been modified to respect confidentiality.

growth plans. Up to that point, little to no investment had been made in marketing. The growth it had experienced had been purely from a sales play, and it wasn't growing nearly as fast as its founder had planned. Reality simply wasn't aligning with his bold vision for the firm.

Its CEO, Tim, approached us for a market research and strategy build engagement to jump-start its marketing efforts. After our project kicked off, during some of the early discovery meetings with Tim, he finally disclosed some deep reservations. Being in such a relationship-based niche, Tim was skeptical about marketing and unsure if the engineers AI-Lift sold to were really "susceptible" to marketing. He admitted he was engaging in this market research project to satisfy a request by his board chair.

Through the market research process, our team uncovered a deep desire among the company's engineering customer base for more technical specifications and product shots online to aid in their purchase decisions. They wanted to be informed about product enhancements on a far more regular basis. They wanted to see the sophistication of the sales team leveled up. They felt that AI-Lift's brand identity wasn't nearly of the caliber of its products, and it influenced their decision to buy. In fact, its customers were buying more products from AI-Lift's top two competitors than they were from AI-Lift themselves. The marketing plan basically wrote itself. Even with all the branding and website development work—elements that tend to have a long payout—to be completed in year one, the projected MROI that first year would have been $4:$1.

Despite the promising outlook and a guaranteed plan, Tim chose not to implement the strategy, hesitant to rely on marketing data over his understanding of his customer base. The high CAC, which our plan projected to halve, remained unchanged. This case serves as a reminder of the importance of embracing data-driven strategies to realize untapped growth potential. I implore you, as a marketing leader or CEO, to consider the all-too-often truth that you likely don't know your customers as well as you think you do. It's that beautiful passion that creates bias.

> **START A REVOLUTION: ACKNOWLEDGE THAT YOU DON'T REALLY KNOW THY CUSTOMER.**

12 BATTLES™ FRAMEWORK

1 YOU **ACCEPT** THAT YOU DESERVE AND WILL ACHIEVE GUARANTEED MARKETING OUTCOMES.

2 YOU **ACKNOWLEDGE** THAT YOU DON'T REALLY KNOW THY CUSTOMER.

3 YOU **CHAMPION** MARKET RESEARCH AS A DO-OR-DIE INVESTMENT.

4 YOU **EMBRACE** THE POWER OF ATTRIBUTION MODELING AND STOP ACCEPTING BAD DATA.

5 YOU **OWN** AN OPENING IN THE BRANDSCAPE.

6 YOU **TORCH** YOUR EXISTING STRATEGY UNAPOLOGETICALLY IF NEEDED.

7 YOU **ADVOCATE** FOR AN INVESTMENT IN EACH STAGE OF THE CUSTOMER JOURNEY.

8 YOU **CHALLENGE** YOUR TEAM TO MAKE POWERFUL STRATEGIC SHIFTS GROUNDED IN RESEARCH VERSUS TRADITION.

9 YOU **PREACH** THE GOOD WORD OF DISCIPLINED OPTIMIZATION.

10 YOU **COMMIT** TO BUILDING A PAY-FOR-PERFORMANCE TEAM AROUND YOUR STRATEGY; NOT VICE VERSA.

11 YOU **REQUIRE** A POWERFUL MARKETING DASHBOARD AND DOCUMENTED PROCESSES.

12 YOU **INSPIRE** YOUR TEAM TO STAND BEHIND THEIR MROI PROJECTIONS.

BATTLE 3 : YOU **CHAMPION** MARKET RESEARCH AS A DO-OR-DIE INVESTMENT

Battle 3

Battle 3 calls for you to champion market research as a do-or-die investment.

This deep analysis is not just an expense; it's an invaluable investment in the future success and sustainability of your business. Market research informs decision making, mitigates risks, and helps identify opportunities.

As discussed in Battle 2, you are inherently biased. So when it comes to research, you need a great deal of objectivity, and the best way to achieve this objectivity is to outsource your market research. If you are not in a position to outsource your market research, conduct your own with at least an external objective advisor. But don't pick and choose only the research elements your team has the time or expertise to execute. It's more important to complete the research in full than for it to be perfect. You cannot shortcut market research and have any hope of reliably predicting outcomes.

> **YOU CANNOT SHORTCUT MARKET RESEARCH AND HAVE ANY HOPE OF RELIABLY PREDICTING YOUR OUTCOMES.**

Research as an Imperative

Based on my experience over the last two decades, most people reading this book are wasting 60 percent of their marketing investment a year. If you spend $100,000 annually on marketing, that's $60,000 being wasted every year, and a $300,000 misspend over five years. You can generally outsource this entire research protocol for roughly $30,000 to $65,000, and most of it will last you, on average, five years depending on how dynamic your industry is. The bottom line is you can't afford to skip market research. It's the primary driver of your ability to drive strong, predictable marketing outcomes.

> **FOR MOST OF YOU READING THIS BOOK, YOU ARE WASTING A FULL 60 PERCENT OF YOUR MARKETING INVESTMENT A YEAR. YOU CAN'T AFFORD TO SKIP MARKET RESEARCH. IT'S THE PRIMARY DRIVER OF YOUR ABILITY TO DRIVE STRONG, PREDICTABLE MARKETING OUTCOMES.**

The majority of marketing leaders and CEOs I've worked with over the years came to the table skeptical about the need for market research. I've heard hundreds of variations of "Why wouldn't I just put that money into execution?" I get it. If you haven't seen the power of market research firsthand, disbelief is natural. If you cannot let go of that thinking, however, and embrace quality research as the linchpin to predictable marketing, your odds of success drop substantially.

There are two types of research protocols—qualitative and quantitative—and utilizing both gives you the greatest advantage when building an informed results-guaranteed marketing strategy.

Qualitative research is used to determine the scope of beliefs about your brand and its place in the market that must later be vetted against a statistically valid audience size—which is your quantitative research. This quantitative vetting is necessary to ensure you have sufficient clarity and ammunition to craft a strategy with predictable outcomes. Think of qualitative research as the perceptions, opinions, and viewpoints that must be validated statistically through the hard numbers, which are your quantitative methods. Your research protocol generally should include the following elements.

Qualitative research protocol
1. Internal and external stakeholder interviews
2. Competitive surveillance including reputation scan and indexing
3. Value proposition comparison
4. Offer strategy evaluation
5. Sales and marketing alignment inventory

Quantitative research protocol
1. Marketing performance audit
2. Customer transaction analysis
3. Current, lost, and prospective customer survey

Qualitative Research: Internal and External Stakeholder Interviews

The first step when conducting qualitative research is to administer individual interviews with your key internal and external stakeholders. This allows you to see where their views and perspectives align and differ. Internal stakeholders typically include your leadership team, your board, and a sampling of frontline employees who engage with your customers directly, including customer service, sales, and marketing. External stakeholders typically include current customers, lost customers, and prospective customers. As with all qualitative research, your big picture objective is to identify the boundaries of hypotheses and perspectives that you will later vet against a statistically valid audience—predominantly in your customer and prospective customer surveys. These interviews are a versatile and potent qualitative research method that offer a clear picture of what your internal and external stakeholders believe and why. Broadly speaking, these interviews seek to understand the company's perceived strengths, differentiators, competitive landscape, motivations of targeted customers, opportunities and obstacles for growth, and any limiting beliefs.

Internal Stakeholder Interview Objectives

Clear research objectives help focus the interview and ensure that you gather relevant information. They guide the entire research process and help you stay on track. Clear objectives outline what you want your research to accomplish. For example:

- Who your competition is and how you stack up against them—in your differentiators, products and services, and sales and marketing strategies.

- Who your ideal customer is—from demographics to psycho-graphics. What drives them, inspires them, and motivates them to buy?

- Why customers choose you versus your competitors. What would make them choose you more? What is your market share?

- Where your operations, sales, and marketing teams are in alignment and where they aren't. Where does sales and marketing messaging vary? Where does sales and marketing messaging differ from the reality of what you deliver?

- What your brand identity is. How do customers perceive your brand?

- Where there are openings in the market you're not fully realizing. These could be new verticals or targeted customers or alternate positioning/differentiation opportunities.

The best practice is to develop custom interview guides for each person you'll be interviewing. At a minimum, you'll want distinct questions for the C-Suite, marketing, sales, customer service, and operations. Plan for hour-long interviews with generally 10 to 15 questions per interview.

CHECK OUT THE 12 BATTLES™ READER HUB at marketingtoolsforyou.com for this free resource:

INTERNAL STAKEHOLDER INTERVIEW GUIDE TEMPLATE

External Stakeholder Interview Objectives

Your external stakeholder interview objectives are generally to learn your *customers' and lost customers'* views on:

- Who they believe you compete with and why they chose you over your competitors.

- What share of wallet they are investing with you as compared to your competitors.

- What they believe your real differentiators to be and how those differences stack up against the competition.

- What you could do to earn more of their business.

- What would drive them to purchase more from a competitor.

- What problems or pain they have that you could be solving.

- Why they no longer do business with you, including any reasons they were hesitant to share with your team, and what you could do to earn their business back.

Your external stakeholder interview objectives are also to learn your *prospective customers'* views on:

- Who they believe you compete with and why they chose your competitors over you.

- What they believe your real differentiators to be and how those differences stack up against the competition.

- What you could do to take their business from your competitor, including what they're spending currently with your competitor.

- What problems or pain their current supplier is not delivering on.

- What your competitors do well on the sales and marketing front.

The best practice is to develop custom interview guides for your current, lost, and prospective customer interviews. Plan for hour-long interviews with generally 10 to 15 questions per interview.

CHECK OUT THE 12 BATTLES™ READER HUB at marketingtoolsforyou.com for this free resource:

EXTERNAL STAKEHOLDER INTERVIEW GUIDE TEMPLATE

Stakeholder Interview Best Practices

Follow these best practices to conduct effective internal and external stakeholder interviews.

Determine the right interview quantity: With internal interviews, look for 5 to 10 total stakeholders. With external interviews, look for 10 to 20 stakeholders. These ranges provide a balance between depth and breadth. Any fewer and a single outlier could notably sway the results.

Select the right stakeholders: Identifying and involving the appropriate stakeholders ensures that you are collecting information from those who have the most direct or significant involvement or interest in the growth of your company. Be sure to include people with views different from the internal norm, as this stage of research is not about validating current thinking but about exploring unrealized potential.

BE SURE TO INCLUDE PEOPLE WITH VIEWS DIFFERENT FROM THE INTERNAL NORM, AS THIS STAGE OF RESEARCH IS NOT ABOUT VALIDATING CURRENT THINKING BUT ABOUT EXPLORING WHAT COULD BE.

Provide context to the stakeholders: Offering context about the research, its purpose, and the expected outcomes helps stakeholders understand the significance of their input. It encourages their participation and cooperation. Explain that the purpose of the research is to help you stay connected to what matters most to your customers and the market, and that their candor will be enormously valuable. Make sure they understand that their individual responses will be kept confidential.

Have a structured interview guide: A structured guide ensures the interview questions are consistent and bias-free, making it easier to compare and analyze the responses. Questions should be grouped by category of questions and customized by role (e.g., leadership, front line) or customer type (e.g., current, past, or prospective).

Ask open-ended questions: Open-ended questions encourage stakeholders to provide detailed, unscripted responses. This allows for a richer exploration of their perspectives and experiences rather than simple "yes" or "no" answers.

Engage in active listening: Active listening is crucial to fully understanding stakeholders' responses. It involves not only hearing their words but also observing non-verbal cues and showing empathy and respect. Be careful not to interrupt, and never help the interviewee answer the question. You must remain an unbiased observer.

Probe for details: Follow-up questions or probes can uncover deeper insights or clarify vague responses. This technique ensures a comprehensive understanding of the stakeholder's viewpoint. If you feel you're getting superficial responses, say "tell me more" as many times as needed until you are satisfied with the depth and breadth of the response.

Offer confidentiality: Ensuring the confidentiality of the interview responses creates a safe space for stakeholders to express their views honestly, especially if the topic is sensitive or contentious.

Gather diverse perspectives: Including a variety of stakeholders with different roles, experiences, tenure, and viewpoints provides a more holistic understanding of the topic. Diverse perspectives can lead to more robust and well-rounded findings. For external interviews, be sure to include current and lost customers; ideal customers as well as those who aren't ideal but should be based on their profile; long-standing and new customers; big spenders and small ones; those who buy exclusively from you and those who spend little with you; and, finally, prospective customers who are both active in your pipeline as well as those who previously chose not to buy.

Record the interview: Recording the interview, with the stakeholder's consent, is essential for accuracy. It allows you to review and transcribe responses, ensuring that you don't miss critical details. It also allows you to be entirely present in each interview rather than focusing on your note taking. Note taking also distracts from your ability to read non-verbal cues. There are numerous low-cost platforms that will automatically transcribe your recorded content.

Leverage the bridging technique: It can be challenging to keep these conversations on track. Use the bridging technique to steer the discussion back on track if it digresses. This ensures you cover the necessary topics while respecting the stakeholder's perspective. The bridging technique involves acknowledging the current topic and then gently redirecting the interviewee to the topic at hand. It's a conversational pivot—acknowledge, bridge, and steer. For instance, if a stakeholder veers off-topic, you might say, "That's an interesting point (acknowledge), and it brings us back (bridge) to what we were discussing earlier about [subject] (steer)." This method keeps the conversation respectful and focused without dismissing the interviewee's thoughts.

Conduct analysis and document: Thoroughly analyzing and documenting the interview data is the final step in completing your stakeholder interviews. Your goal is to identify any topics worth exploring in greater detail via follow-up interviews and, ultimately, key themes worth exploring in the quantitative research.

Incorporating these best practices into your stakeholder interviews helps you conduct more rigorous and insightful research, ultimately leading to better-informed decisions, policies, or solutions based on a deeper understanding of stakeholder perspectives and needs.

Stakeholder Interview Pitfalls to Avoid

Avoid these pitfalls in internal and external stakeholder interviews to ensure the validity and credibility of your research.

Avoid leading questions: For example, "Do you believe the most valuable benefit we offer is high-quality products?" The way this question is asked lends itself to a "yes" or "no" response rather than more detailed feedback, greatly limiting the kind of data you will gather. Leading questions can bias the responses by suggesting a preferred answer and can manipulate or influence the stakeholder's viewpoint, which undermines the integrity of the interview. A non-leading version of this question is, "What do you believe is the most valuable benefit we offer customers?"

Don't make assumptions: Making assumptions about what stakeholders might say or believe can lead to confirmation bias, where you only hear what you expect to hear and disregard dissenting opinions or novel insights.

Avoid bias: Whether it's based on personal opinions or preconceived notions, interview bias can skew the interview process and lead to a misrepresentation of stakeholder perspectives. For example, often interviewers assume that a new employee or customer gives incomplete or uninformed answers. In some cases, newer team members and customers have a more objective point of view than individuals who have been part of the business on the employer side or customer side for a while.

> WHETHER IT'S BASED ON PERSONAL OPINIONS OR PRECONCEIVED NOTIONS, INTERVIEW BIAS CAN SKEW THE INTERVIEW PROCESS AND LEAD TO A MISREPRESENTATION OF STAKEHOLDER PERSPECTIVES.

Avoid inactive listening: Failing to actively listen means missing important nuances, emotions, or key information that stakeholders may convey, resulting in incomplete or inaccurate data.

Avoid interrupting or rushing: Interrupting the interviewee when they are speaking and/or rushing through the interview can leave your stakeholders feeling disrespected and may deter them from fully sharing their thoughts, hindering the research process. Instead, set aside enough time (roughly one hour) for a thorough interview process and prioritize your question guide from most to least important in case you don't get through them all.

Avoid question overload: Too many questions in a short period can overwhelm interviewees, causing them to provide superficial or incomplete responses. Prioritize questions and space them out effectively. A properly spaced interview begins with a couple of easy questions to warm up the interviewee and spreads the most complex questions throughout the interview. Generally speaking, look at 10 to 15 questions maximum in a one-hour interview.

Don't miss opportunities for clarity: If you don't seek clarification when an answer is unclear or ambiguous, it can lead to misinterpretation or inaccurate data analysis. For example, if two stakeholders each said the company's strongest differentiator is their products, one could have easily meant the overall quality of those products while the other meant the unique functionality. Remember to wear your unbiased observer hat and ask questions as if you're new to the business.

Don't miss non-verbal cues: Body language and facial expressions can provide valuable context and emotional nuances. When you see a non-verbal cue you aren't clear about, ask. Disregarding them can lead to missing vital information. When asking about non-verbal cues, be sensitive to how you position the question. For example, if you notice that an interviewee from the sales team seems frustrated with a question about what is contributing to the company's low close rates and doesn't seem to be sharing their full views on the matter, consider saying, "I can tell you're passionate about the company, and I'm sure with your experience, you have ideas for how the company can improve on this front. Tell me more." Don't call out what you recognize as frustration; simply dig into the heart of the matter using my favorite interview statement of all: "Tell me more."

Don't be rigid: Get comfortable with the questions in advance and allow the interview to assume a natural flow. A rigid script can stifle the organic percolation of conversation and prevent you from exploring unexpected insights or follow-up questions.

Don't bias your sample: A biased sample, such as only your most profitable customers or your most tenured employees, can result in skewed findings that do not accurately represent the diverse perspectives of stakeholders. A random or well-considered sample is more representative. Bottom line: Look for diversity of participants.

Don't forget to offer confidentiality: Failing to ensure confidentiality can deter stakeholders from participating openly and honestly.

Don't ignore or get defensive when faced with negative feedback: Negative feedback can be valuable for improving policies, products, or services. Ignoring it can lead to missed opportunities for growth and improvement. Don't get defensive if you hear dissenting views. Instead, get curious.

Qualitative Research: Competitive Surveillance Including Reputation Scan and Indexing

How can you possibly navigate the most cost-effective methods for taking market share from your competitors if you don't keep tabs on their movements? Some light and perfectly legal surveillance is in order.

There are SaaS (software as a service) platforms that allow you to monitor the digital marketing movements and investments of your competitors in addition to conducting competitor reputation scans. A reputation scan is an analysis of the keywords that the market is using to talk about your competitors with the purpose of identifying actionable trends.

There are numerous low-cost competitive intelligence platforms that can be leveraged for:

- Keyword research, backlink tracking, and other SEO (search engine optimization) analysis.

- Website traffic analysis and audience insight tools including content tracking.

- Email monitoring.

- Social media comparisons.

- Brand reputation and customer review monitoring.

CHECK OUT THE 12 BATTLES™ READER HUB at marketingtoolsforyou.com for this free resource:

COMPETITIVE INTELLIGENCE PLATFORMS

With these insights in hand, synthesize the data into an index that ranks the strength of each of your competitors in each of the primary marketing channels used in your industry so that you have a cheat sheet, similar to the following, for quick reference regarding which competitors you're going head-to-head with in each space. This index will also indicate gaps in their strategies—such as a channel where your customers are but your most serious competition largely isn't. And that's an opportunity to steal market share.

SAMPLE COMPETITVE INDEX

SOCIAL MEDIA ADS	LINK TO META AD LIBRARY	LINK TO LINKEDIN AD LIBRARY	NUMBER OF ADS	RANKING 1-5
Your Company				
Competitor A				
Competitor B				
Competitor C				
Competitor D				

SOCIAL MEDIA FOLLLOWERS	FACEBOOK	INSTAGRAM	X/ TWITTER	LINKEDIN	PINTEREST	TOTAL	RANKING 1-5
Your Company							
Competitor A							
Competitor B							
Competitor C							
Competitor D							

SEO STRATEGY	DOMAIN AUTHORITY	LINKING ROOT DOMAIN	SITE RANKING	NUMBER OF RANKING KEYWORDS	NUMBER OF KEYWORDS IN 1-3 POSITIONS	NUMBER OF KEYWORDS IN 4-10 POSITIONS	RANKING 1-5
Your Company							
Competitor A							
Competitor B							
Competitor C							
Competitor D							

SAMPLE COMPETITVE INDEX

TECH STACK	CONTENT MANAGEMENT	MARKETING AUTOMATION	ANALYTICS	CONTENT/SOCIAL	RANKING 1-5
Your Company					
Competitor A					
Competitor B					
Competitor C					
Competitor D					

WEBSITE CONVERSION POINTS	PRIMARY CTA (HOME PAGE)	TOP OF FUNNEL CONVERSION POINTS	MIDDLE OF FUNNEL CONVERSION POINTS	BOTTOM OF FUNNEL CONVERSION POINTS	RANKING 1-5
Your Company					
Competitor A					
Competitor B					
Competitor C					
Competitor D					

CONTENT STRATEGY	BLOG	EBOOKS / WHITE PAPERS	VIDEOS / WEBINARS	AUDIO / PODCASTS	RANKING 1-5
Your Company					
Competitor A					
Competitor B					
Competitor C					
Competitor D					

CHECK OUT THE 12 BATTLES™ READER HUB at marketingtoolsforyou.com for this free resource:

COMPETITIVE INDEX

Qualitative Research: Value Proposition Comparison

Your marketing simply won't work without a compelling value proposition that outlines what sets you apart from your competitors, as well as the unique benefits of your product, service, or solution. And what sets you apart must really matter to your target market. That's the harsh reality that every company must face. Use a value proposition comparison grid to see how yours stacks up in the market.

> **YOUR MARKETING SIMPLY WON'T WORK WITHOUT A COMPELLING VALUE PROPOSITION THAT OUTLINES WHAT SETS YOU APART FROM YOUR COMPETITORS. THAT'S THE HARSH REALITY THAT EVERY COMPANY MUST FACE.**

To build a value proposition comparison grid, start by identifying the key factors that matter to your customers. These could be price, quality, service, speed of delivery, or other USPs (unique selling points) of your products or services. Next, list your company and your three main competitors and rate each one against these factors on a 1 to 10 scale where 10 is high.

B2B mystery shopping involves evaluating competitors as an anonymous potential customer to assess their customer experience, responsiveness, and overall offering. Alternatively, you can ask friends or colleagues outside of your company to conduct these assessments for you. It's worth the time investment as this valuable information can significantly enhance your understanding of the competitive landscape.

SAMPLE VALUE PROPOSITION COMPARISON GRID

UNIQUE SELLING POINTS	YOUR COMPANY 1-10	COMPETITOR A 1-10	COMPETITOR B 1-10	COMPETITOR C 1-10
Price				
Quality				
Customer Service				
Innovation				
Brand Recognition				
Product Range				
Technology				
User Experience				
Customization				
After-Sales Support				

A vitally important step is to gather feedback from actual customers about the grid. What do they agree and disagree with? You can do this through a survey to customers or phone interviews. Be sure to select customers you can count on for their candor. Also, be sure to update this regularly because markets evolve and competition shifts.

This grid will visually illustrate where you lead or lag in the market and guide strategic decisions to enhance your value proposition where it counts.

CHECK OUT THE 12 BATTLES™ READER HUB at marketingtoolsforyou.com for this free resource:

VALUE PROPOSITION COMPARISON GRID

Qualitative Research: Offer Strategy Evaluation

Even the strongest marketing strategy will be in vain if the offer strategy isn't compelling to your specific target audience, which is why it's important to objectively assess how your offer strategy stacks up when compared to those of your competitors—based both on your customers' needs and desires and your competitors' offers.

To effectively evaluate and structure an offer strategy, consider the following steps:

1. **Map your offers across the customer journey:** Where do your offers currently fit into each of the four stages of the customer journey—awareness, consideration, conversion, and the post-purchase experience? What value-add or free offers/content do you already make available to prospective customers

who are in the awareness stage—those just getting to know your brand? What low-cost trial offers do you make available when they are in the consideration stage, where they may be comparing you to your competition? What offers are available for those wanting to make a first purchase of size with your company? And what offers are available to existing customers to retain them and encourage additional purchases?

CUSTOMER JOURNEY

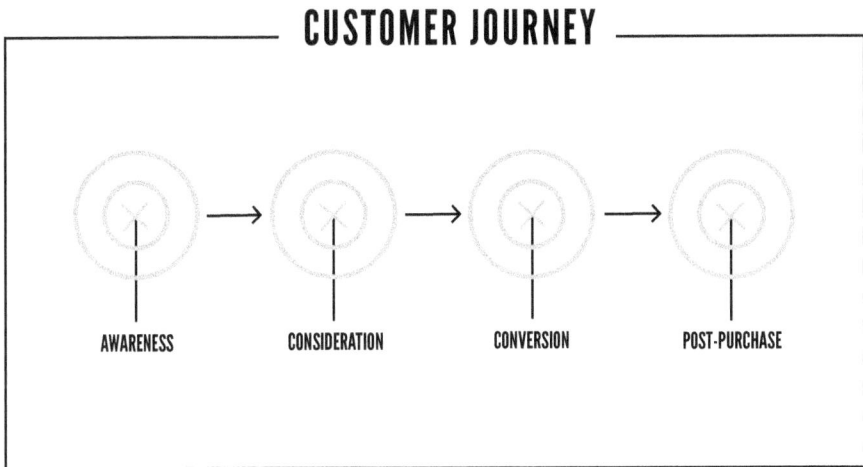

AWARENESS   CONSIDERATION   CONVERSION   POST-PURCHASE

2. **Consider ascending offers:** Next, consider improving your offer strategy by creating tiers of offers that increase in value, complexity, or commitment, starting from an entry-level proposition to the most premium package. This is called an ascending offer or value-ladder strategy. Be sure the step from "never purchased" to "first purchase" is not too steep; make it easy for a brand-new customer to give you that initial "yes" with a reasonable ask and price point. The idea is to begin with a free or ultra-low-cost lead-generating offer designed to build interest in your brand while your prospect is in the awareness stage of the customer journey. Then, as your customer enters the consideration stage, progress to an initial offer that you perhaps break even on that

gives your prospect an opportunity to get to know your brand before making a big commitment. Once they get to know you, move them into the conversion stage with your primary offer. Once they're a loyal customer, as part of the post-purchase experience, offer them your exclusive VIP offer available only to your best customers. I'll illustrate how RedRover structures its ascending offer strategy with pricing slowly ascending as a client gains more familiarity with the firm:

a. **Free lead magnets:** Lead-magnets are designed to be free value-add offers to prospective customers. RedRover's current lead magnets are twofold: access to the 12 Battles™ Readiness Assessment followed by an invitation to view our Marketing Results Guaranteed Webinar.

b. **Initial break-even offer:** Webinar attendees are then invited to participate in a Marketing Clarity Assessment, which is a deep-dive marketing audit, as a way to allow prospective clients to get to know the team before making a sizable investment.

c. **Primary offers:** Marketing Clarity Assessment participants will receive three primary offers for building a results-guaranteed marketing strategy, each designed to meet them where they are—whether they are prepared to go it alone, would prefer to collaborate, or elect to outsource it all:

i. The DIY (do it yourself) offer: An on-demand version of our Marketing Results Guaranteed BootCamp consisting of 18 hours of recorded content that teaches the client's team how to research and build their own results-guaranteed marketing strategy.

ii. DWY (do it with you) offer: A live version of the Marketing Results Guaranteed BootCamp followed by an invitation to join our Marketing Results Guaranteed MasterMind group for weekly training, coaching, and accountability.

iii. DFY (do it for you) offer: An option to outsource the entire research, strategy, and execution effort by engaging RedRover for its GO (growth optimization) Plan service.

d. **Exclusive VIP Offers:** Where there is a fit, GO Plan and MasterMind attendees are invited to join a Quarterly Strategic Innovation Council or the Joint Venture Program—RedRover's two exclusive VIP offers.

As you can see, the key to the ascending offer strategy is to earn the right to larger customer engagements by building trust along the way.

> CONSIDER IMPROVING YOUR OFFER STRATEGY BY CREATING TIERS OF OFFERS THAT INCREASE IN VALUE, COMPLEXITY, OR COMMITMENT, STARTING FROM AN ENTRY-LEVEL PROPOSITION TO THE MOST PREMIUM PACKAGE. THIS IS CALLED AN ASCENDING OFFER OR VALUE-LADDER STRATEGY.

THE VALUE LADDER

VALUE

Exclusive VIP Offer

Primary Offer

Initial Break-Even Offer

Free Lead Magnet

PRICE

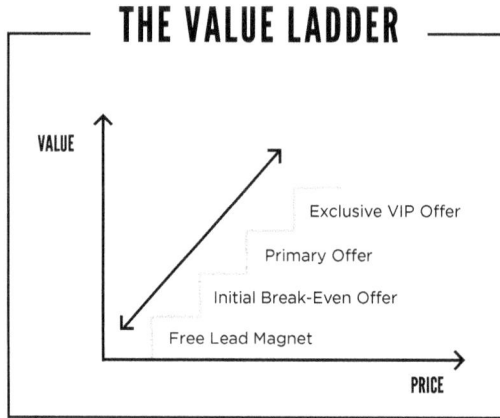

3. **Analyze competitor tiers:** Look at how competitors structure their ascending offers and identify opportunities or gaps you can fill. You can do this by visiting their websites or through mystery shopping.

4. **Align with customer desires:** Ensure each ascending offer addresses evolving customer needs more comprehensively as they move up the tiers. For instance, if you're in the B2B software industry, your customer interviews and surveys may reveal that as businesses grow, they require more advanced features, scalability, and dedicated customer support. Tailoring your higher-tier offerings to meet these evolving B2B needs can enhance your value proposition and customer satisfaction.

5. **Create an inventory:**

   a. The vertical axis lists the stages of the customer journey (awareness, consideration, conversion, post-purchase) and the corresponding tiers of the offer (e.g., lead magnet, initial break-even, primary, and exclusive VIP).

   b. The horizontal axis features customer needs, your offers, and your competitors' offers at each tier.

c. Evaluate how each offer aligns with customer expectations and how it stands against competitors at every level.

SAMPLE ASCENDING OFFER STRATEGY INVENTORY

CUSTOMER JOURNEY STAGE WITH CORRESPONDING ASCENDING OFFERS	CUSTOMER NEEDS	YOUR OFFERS	COMPETITOR A OFFERS	COMPETITOR B OFFERS
Awareness Lead magnet offers				
Consideration Initial break-even offers				
Conversion Primary offers				
Post-Purchase Exclusive VIP offers				

Using this matrix, you can pinpoint where to enhance your offers to guide customers organically to higher levels of engagement and investment by crafting a compelling offer at every stage.

CHECK OUT THE 12 BATTLES™ READER HUB at marketingtoolsforyou.com for this free resource:

ASCENDING OFFER STRATEGY INVENTORY

Qualitative Research: Sales and Marketing Alignment Inventory

When I founded RedRover, the commitment I made to myself was to always ensure my team was in alignment with our clients' sales teams because I had seen first-hand how much marketing investment waste occurs when these components are out of sync. In one of my enterprise marketing experiences, my new marketing team was generating leads, but they weren't aligned with the sales team's ideal customer profile. This resulted in a disconnect and wasted resources. In another company, I found that proper alignment between marketing and sales teams led to a significant increase in referrals and revenue growth.

> **THE COMMITMENT I MADE TO MYSELF WAS TO ALWAYS ENSURE MY TEAM WAS IN ALIGNMENT WITH OUR CLIENTS' SALES TEAMS BECAUSE I HAD SEEN FIRST-HAND HOW MUCH MARKETING INVESTMENT WASTE OCCURS WHEN THEY ARE OUT OF SYNC.**

To assess how well your sales and marketing teams are aligned, put together a sales and marketing alignment inventory to identify the primary gaps you can tackle one by one. To build this inventory, assess your teams on the following fronts.

Communication: Evaluate the frequency and effectiveness of communication between sales and marketing. Are there regular meetings? Is there a clear exchange of information?

Shared goals: Check if both departments have common objectives. Are they working toward the same KPIs including the same revenue or gross profit targets?

Customer understanding: Ensure both teams have a congruous understanding of the customer profile and buyer journey.

Content usage: Look at how sales uses marketing content. Is it integral to their process, and is it effective? Does the sales messaging mirror the marketing messaging? Does marketing seek regular feedback from sales on their messaging?

Feedback loop: Assess if there's a system for sales to provide feedback on leads and if marketing acts on this feedback.

CRM utilization: Examine whether both sales and marketing are using the CRM effectively and if the data is shared and up to date.

Lead handling: Review the process for lead management. How are leads qualified by marketing? How effective is the handover of leads from marketing to sales? How are the leads requalified by sales, and how effective is the follow up from sales?

To complete the inventory, use the template that follows. Provide a score from 1 to 10 next to each category to indicate alignment, where 1 indicates very poor alignment and 10 indicates excellent alignment.

SAMPLE SALES AND MARKETING ALIGNMENT INVENTORY

SALES AND MARKETING ALIGNMENT CATEGORIES	SCORE (1-10)	NOTES
Communication		
Shared Goals		
Customer Understanding		
Content Usage		
Feedback Loop		
CRM Utilization		
Lead Handling		

Use this template in regular (monthly or quarterly) alignment meetings to identify gaps and develop action plans to address them.

CHECK OUT THE 12 BATTLES™ READER HUB at marketingtoolsforyou.com for this free resource:

SALES AND MARKETING ALIGNMENT INVENTORY

If you want a high-performance marketing plan, both your sales and marketing teams need to be performing optimally. In addition to team alignment, it's equally important that you have the right sales process, the right salespeople wired for sales success, and the right sales incentive plan—all compatible with one another and in alignment with growth goals. When these departments work cohesively and collaboratively, your overall business performance is enhanced.

CHECK OUT THE 12 BATTLES™ READER HUB at marketingtoolsforyou.com for this free resource:

SALES PROCESS/PEOPLE/COMP PLAN EVALUATION BEST PRACTICES

Quantitative Research: Marketing Performance Audit

Your first piece of quantitative analysis should be an audit of the performance of your own marketing strategy—an objective break-down of what has and hasn't worked during the previous year; which investments paid off and which were wasted; which strategies require additional testing and which you should torch; and, most importantly, where there are optimizations that could boost your MROI. It's important that your audit compares your performance to both industry benchmarks and your own performance over time.

Branding and Messaging
Before you dig into your detailed analysis, begin by assessing the overall effectiveness of your branding and messaging.

Your branding and messaging play a significant role in shaping customer perceptions. Assess how well they resonate with your target audience. Does your positioning break through with your target market? Is it contributing to brand loyalty? Is it driving conversions? To determine this, evaluate the consistency of your messaging across channels and how well it aligns with the needs and values of your audience by asking them in your upcoming customer and prospect survey. Examine conversion rates and attribution data to understand how your messaging influences customer decision making and the overall conversion process.

Marketing Disciplines

Next, assess your marketing performance by discipline. Compare your results to the previous year's baseline to help you assess growth or regression. Benchmark against industry standards and competitors to gain insights into your relative position. Disciplines to evaluate include:

Website

- **Website traffic:** Measure the number of visitors, page views, and unique visitors.

- **Conversion rate:** Track the percentage of website visitors who take a desired action, such as making a purchase or filling out a contact form.

- **Heat map:** Track visitors' website behavior based on where they most commonly click and scroll on your site through a process called heat mapping, which uses visual overlays to highlight the areas of highest user engagement. This visual representation helps you identify which sections of your website attract the most attention and which may need optimization.

SEO

- **Organic search traffic:** Measure the number of visitors who find your website through unpaid search results.

- **Keyword rankings:** Track the position of your website for important keywords.

- **CTR (click-through rate):** Monitor the percentage of users who click on your search engine listings.

- **Lead generation:** Track the number of leads generated through organic marketing efforts.

The most efficient way to track your SEO performance is to leverage a comprehensive SEO analytics tool that can provide a centralized dashboard where you can monitor organic search traffic, keyword rankings, CTR, and lead generation metrics in real time.

Content marketing

- **Content engagement:** Measure how users interact with your content, such as time on page and social shares. Understand which medium is driving traffic to your most important content pages.

- **Lead generation:** Track the number of leads generated through content marketing efforts.

Social media (assess the following for each platform)

- **Follower growth:** Measure the increase in followers on social media platforms.

- **Engagement rate:** Monitor likes, comments, shares, and clicks on social media posts.

- **Conversion rate:** Track the percentage of social media users who take a desired action, such as signing up for a newsletter.

- **Lead generation:** Track the number of leads generated through organic social media efforts.

- **Social media advertising:** If you're running paid social media ads, evaluate the following:

  - **Ad impressions:** Measure how often your ads are viewed.

  - **CTR:** Monitor the percentage of users who click on your social media ads.

  - **Conversion rate:** Track the percentage of ad clicks that result in a desired action, such as completing an online form.

Email marketing

- **Open rate:** Measure the percentage of email recipients who open your emails.

- **CTR:** Monitor the percentage of email recipients who click on links within your emails.

- **Conversion rate:** Track the percentage of email recipients who complete a desired action, such as making a purchase.

PPC (pay-per-click) advertising

- **CTR:** Monitor the percentage of users who click on your ads.

- **Conversion rate:** Track the percentage of ad clicks that result in a desired action, such as downloading a free online resource from your site.

- **ROAS (return on ad spend):** Measure the revenue generated for every dollar spent on advertising.

- **Search impression share:** Measure the share of targeted searches you receive.

Marketing automation

- **New lead volume:** Measure how many total unique new leads visit your website.

- **Customer journey progression:** Measure how leads move through the ideal user journey experience—the results of which are evidenced by the conversion rate at each of your ascending offer tiers.

- **Email campaign performance:** Monitor the effectiveness of email campaigns in nurturing leads through this marketing funnel.

- **MQLs (marketing qualified leads: leads that have engaged with company marketing efforts and are deemed to be more likely to make a purchase than other leads):** Track the number of leads that meet specific criteria and are ready for sales engagement.

When my team conducts Marketing Clarity Assessments for our clients, we are struck by how often there is misalignment between the strategies and channels where a company spends and those that most effectively drive sales. Armed with the data-driven insights from our assessments, we help each company reallocate its budget toward the marketing strategies that will reap more profitable outcomes.

Pitfalls
When building your marketing performance audit, be sure to avoid these four common pitfalls.

Avoid making excuses: Allowing your team to make excuses for underperforming marketing efforts can hinder progress. Instead of identifying areas for improvement, this approach deflects responsibility and prevents constructive analysis and improvement. An honest assessment of marketing performance allows for the identification of issues and the development of strategies to overcome challenges.

Avoid bias: A lack of objectivity can lead to a biased analysis and skewed perspective, which may result in the misinterpretation of data or the reinforcement of preconceived notions and potentially flawed decision making. Avoid assumptions and evaluate data and outcomes impartially or hire a market research partner to do it for you.

Don't skip the benchmarks: Without benchmarking against industry standards or competitors, it's challenging to gauge the relative performance of marketing efforts. This limits insights into where improvements are needed. Benchmarks provide a basis for comparison and more informed decision making.

Avoid analysis paralysis: Overanalysis, overthinking, and excessive data gathering can lead to indecision and delayed action, which can result in missed opportunities. Effective marketing analysis strikes a balance between thorough examination and timely decision making.

CHECK OUT THE 12 BATTLES™ READER HUB at marketingtoolsforyou.com for this free resource:

MARKETING PERFORMANCE AUDIT TEMPLATE

Quantitative Research: Customer Transaction Analysis

There are 10 primary goals when digging into historical customer transaction data. This analysis should uncover:

1. Your most profitable products or services.

2. The demographics and buying trends of your most profitable customers as well as lookalikes with the potential to be in that tier.

3. Product/service buying trends and how these may vary by geography or customer type.

4. Any seasonality to your business and how this varies by geography and customer type. For example, if you are a distributor of air conditioning components, your peak season is in the warm months, which may begin in May in the Deep South but as late as July in the Northeast.

5. The growth trajectory of every product or service by geography and customer type.

6. How your average transaction values have changed over time.

7. Which segments have delivered in the past and which segments have proven to misfire.

8. Which customer types are spending more or less with you compared to previous years.

9. What your largest dormant customer segment is.

10. What percent of your business is from repeat buyers and whether this is on an incline or decline.

Some of your biggest opportunities for growth will likely come from this data, which is why it's important to adhere to the following best practices.

Clean data before cutting: Data quality is paramount for accurate analysis. Before diving into transaction data analysis, ensure that your data is clean, free from errors, duplicates, and inconsistencies. Clean data is the foundation for reliable insights. Data cleaning involves identifying and rectifying errors, such as missing or incorrect values. It also involves deduplication to eliminate redundant data. Clean data sets the stage for accurate transaction analysis.

Utilize multiple years of data: Sales data from multiple years provides insights into trends and patterns over time. This historical perspective is invaluable for understanding long-term performance. Comparing data across different years helps you identify growth or decline trends, seasonality, and cyclical patterns. This allows for more informed decision making and strategy development. A minimum of five years is recommended.

Leverage segmentation analysis: Segmenting your data into different categories or groups (e.g., by product, region, or customer type) allows you to analyze performance within specific subgroups. This helps uncover insights that may not be apparent in aggregate data. Segmenting data enables you to tailor strategies and make targeted decisions, like identifying high-margin products or customer segments that need more attention.

CHECK OUT THE 12 BATTLES™ READER HUB at marketingtoolsforyou.com for this free resource:

CUSTOMER TRANSACTION ANALYSIS TEMPLATE

Quantitative Research: Current, Lost, and Prospective Customer Survey

To enhance your quantitative research, implement a survey to your existing, former, and potential customers. This crucial step validates your qualitative findings against a statistically significant audience, ensuring your marketing strategy is both predictable and reliable.

Conducting a market survey requires precision. Seeking external expertise for this research will be immensely beneficial to you and offer you deep insights into your customers' characteristics, behaviors, and purchasing habits.

Quantitative research measures the validity of your hypotheses. Surveys statistically confirm, within a margin of error, the likelihood of a customer's decision based on their profile. This method confirms or discounts trends and patterns previously identified through your qualitative research, providing a solid foundation for informed decision making.

Surveys allow you to reach a broader audience than interviews and present a comprehensive understanding of various customer perspectives. They also offer anonymity and encourage honest feedback, which is crucial to identify areas for improvement.

Finally, surveys test your assumptions about customer behavior, supplying concrete data to support or refute your beliefs and, thus, shape effective strategies.

Best Practices
To design effective and actionable surveys that yield results, consider the following best practices.

Determine a credible response rate: It's crucial to define the minimum number of responses required for your survey to have statistical relevance. This ensures that your findings are meaningful and can be confidently used for decision making.

To arrive at the targeted number of responses, you must first determine your minimum acceptable confidence rate and error rate:

- **Survey confidence rate:** This is a measure of how sure you can be that the results of your survey reflect the views of the entire population you're studying. A survey with a 95 percent confidence rate means that you can be 95 percent sure that the results lie within the margin of error.

- **Error rate (margin of error):** This is the range within which the true answer is likely to fall. For example, if you conduct a survey with a margin of error of 5 percent and 80 percent of respondents indicate on the survey that they like a product, the true percentage of people who like the product could be as low as 75 percent or as high as 85 percent. The margin of error acknowledges that there is a chance that the survey results could be off by a small amount.

For statistically valid research, the best practice is to go no lower than a 90 percent confidence level and no higher than a 5 percent margin of error.

The formula for a targeted response rate is complex, so I've provided you with a sample size calculator in the 12 Battles™ Reader Hub. All you need to know is your total audience size—your total number of customers, lost customers, and prospects over the period in which you intend to pull your survey sample. Let's say the period is five years. If you've had 5,000 customers and prospects over five years and you want to maintain a 90 percent confidence rate with a 5 percent error rate, you need results from 259 customers and prospects to complete your survey. If you assume a 20 percent survey response rate from your customers and prospects, you'd need to send the survey to 1,295 customers and prospects, though it's best to give yourself some padding by sending it to at least 50 percent more than you need. In this case, you'd send 1,943 surveys total.

CHECK OUT THE 12 BATTLES™ READER HUB at marketingtoolsforyou.com for this free resource:

SAMPLE SIZE CALCULATOR

Identify the right survey incentives: Offering incentives to survey respondents can boost participation rates and improve the quality of responses. Incentives can be monetary, such as gift cards or discounts; non-monetary, such as charitable contributions, branded gear, and access to exclusive content; or the chance to win a prize. This practice can result in a larger and more diverse respondent pool, leading to more comprehensive and representative data. Be sure to select a survey incentive with universal appeal among your survey population or you could get a biased group of respondents and skew your data.

Consider the survey structure: A well-structured survey is user-friendly and ensures that questions are logically organized. It minimizes respondent confusion and fatigue, making it more likely that respondents will complete it. Proper survey structure includes clear instructions, a logical flow of questions, concise wording, and appropriate survey branching (or skip logic, which changes the next question the respondent sees based on the way the current question is answered), which allows you to tailor the survey experience for individual respondents based on their previous responses. By using branching, you can ask follow-up questions that are directly related to a respondent's earlier answers. This not only reduces survey length, as respondents are only prompted to answer relevant questions, but also makes the survey more engaging and focused on individual preferences or experiences.

Avoid survey bias: Survey bias can lead to skewed results by favoring or disfavoring certain groups or responses. It compromises the survey's objectivity and undermines the accuracy of the data. The two most common types of survey bias are questionnaire bias and sampling bias:

- **Questionnaire bias:** When the wording of questions leads respondents toward a particular answer. Here are the five common types of questionnaire bias:

  - **Leading questions:** Questions that are phrased in a way that suggests a certain answer. For example, "Don't you agree that product X is amazing?" implies that product X is indeed amazing and pushes the respondent to agree.

  - **Loaded questions:** These are questions that contain a controversial or unjustified assumption. For instance, "How problematic do you think the recent pricing changes are?" assumes that the pricing changes are problematic.

  - **Double-barreled questions:** Questions that ask about two things at once, making it unclear which part the respondent is answering. An example is, "How satisfied are you with our pricing and speed of delivery?" The respondent may be satisfied with your pricing but not with your speed of delivery or vice versa.

  - **Absolute questions:** Questions that allow for no degree of variation in responses. For example, "Do you always buy online?" This does not account for occasional changes in routine.

◦ **Order bias:** The sequence of questions or answers can affect responses. If a survey asks a respondent to evaluate a list of product benefits immediately after detailing a common product concern in your industry, the respondent might place undue weight on this product concern in their evaluation. Order bias also can also occur when you don't randomize the order of multiple-choice responses. The response options you list in the first spot or two are likely to be chosen more than those lower on the list. You can set up your survey so that it automatically randomizes the order of the multiple choice options from user to user in order to prevent this.

• **Sampling bias:** Occurs if the survey participants do not accurately represent the larger population. For example, if you only survey your larger or newer customers, you're biasing the survey results. If you take a random sampling of your customer/prospect population, you won't have to worry about this one.

Avoid lengthy surveys: Lengthy surveys lead to survey fatigue, causing respondents to abandon or rush through the survey. This results in incomplete or inaccurate data. Surveys should be concise and focused on essential questions to maintain respondent engagement and data quality.

On average it takes seven and a half seconds to answer an online survey question. If you keep the questions simple, you can ask eight of them in one minute. The best practice is to construct a survey that takes respondents no more than 10 minutes to complete. Five is better.

CHECK OUT THE 12 BATTLES™ READER HUB at marketingtoolsforyou.com for this free resource:

SURVEY LENGTH ESTIMATION CALCULATOR

Include limited open-ended questions: Open-ended questions offer valuable qualitative insights and allow respondents to provide detailed feedback. A survey without open-ended questions may miss essential nuances and context. Incorporating open-ended questions into your survey is important for capturing robust data and understanding the "why" behind quantitative data. However, include too many, and your respondents may get survey fatigue. Use them where you know they'll count, and generally limit them to a maximum of five per survey.

Qualitative and Quantitative: The Right Mix

To craft a results-guaranteed marketing strategy, it's crucial to balance qualitative insights with quantitative analysis. Numbers alone are superficial metrics; they may reveal patterns but not the underlying motivations or sentiments that drive consumer behavior. Relying solely on quantitative data risks overlooking the emotional connections and personal reasons that attract people to a brand or sway them to favor one product over another. Combining quantitative and qualitative data provides a more comprehensive overview of market dynamics. These stories contextualize the statistics, providing a more in-depth understanding of the consumer experience.

> **TO CRAFT A RESULTS-GUARANTEED MARKETING STRATEGY, IT'S CRUCIAL TO BALANCE QUALITATIVE INSIGHTS WITH QUANTITATIVE ANALYSIS.**

However, solely focusing on qualitative data, such as interview anecdotes, can be restrictive. While these narratives are rich in detail, they may not reflect the broader market reality. Decisions based solely on these stories and consumer emotions might resonate with individual experiences but could fail to scale up to larger, statistically significant market trends.

A robust marketing strategy demands a harmonious blend of both data types, allowing for compelling narratives drawn from customer experiences to be validated by quantitative data, ensuring that your strategy resonates with individuals and aligns with the larger market context. The result is a well-rounded, evidence-based marketing strategy with the power to guarantee results.

CHECK OUT THE 12 BATTLES™ READER HUB at marketingtoolsforyou.com for this free resource:

SURVEY QUESTIONNAIRE TEMPLATE

Battle 3 Research Insights[6]

56% is the maximum participation level by survey respondents over the last three years in any of the fundamental market research best practices in which B2B companies should engage. Without this research, a company cannot truly know its customers and competitors to the degree it must to maximize marketing performance.

55% of survey respondents cite "too expensive" as the reason they haven't executed market research over the past three years with 45 percent citing "would rather use those dollars to invest in marketing," which, arguably, also goes to the perceived expense. I contend that it's too expensive not to execute market research.

---

[6] From the "2024 RedRover U.S. Middle-Market B2B Marketing Performance Study," available in the 12 Battles™ Reader Hub at marketingtoolsforyou.com.

Success Story

LegacyTech[7], a $40M family-owned manufacturing company, had been a RedRover client for two years. Its CEO hired my team soon after the marketing director left, asking us to pick up where she had left off.

Two years into the partnership and the plan's performance began to decline. This company had never conducted or allowed us to conduct proper market research into its customer base, its competition, industry trends, etc., so the marketing plan being executed was essentially based on past marketing performance data alone, with a smattering of conjecture. Given the aggressive growth goals of this family company, leadership was open to investing in market research for the first time, so they engaged with RedRover to deploy our signature GO Plan service, which is intensive market research that informs a custom strategy build backed by an MROI guarantee.

We soon learned that LegacyTech's brand positioning had lost relevance; it was seen as the old, stodgy player when it was, in fact, high-tech and innovative. We learned that there were sizable gaps in the PPC strategies of its competitors that we could exploit. We learned that LegacyTech's engineering target market had a strong preference for visual content; historically, 75 percent of the content it produced was in written form. And we learned about the one differentiator that would set it miles apart from its competitors.

Leveraging this new knowledge, we went to work devising a research-backed strategy that we guaranteed would provide significant MROI. Fast-forward a year into the new research-backed plan and closed sales from inbound leads were up over 50 percent (which now comprised nearly 95 percent of the firm's total lead

---

[7] Client details have been modified to respect confidentiality.

volume), and our client was grossly outperforming growth targets. That's the power of research.

Cautionary Tale

Panorama Window and Door[8] is a $30M upscale window and door manufacturing and installation company with offices across the U.S. Historically, little of its lead volume came from marketing; most of its new business came from referrals or from its sales team's outbound efforts.

As the company began to have notable turnover among the sales team in the throes of the Great Resignation[9] post COVID-19, it was ready to invest in a marketing strategy that would drive more consistent lead volume, reduce its reliance on the sales team, and, ultimately, allow it to hire less experienced sales representatives given the lead volume they would receive.

While Panorama didn't have much in the way of historical marketing efforts to assess, there was a critical need to interview and survey customers, lost customers, and prospective customers to better understand the messaging, offer strategy, channels, and positioning that would resonate most with them. As much as the CEO wanted these insights, she was under the gun to reach an annual growth goal set by her board of directors—a growth goal that was aspirational and not based on data—and she only had two more quarters to reach it. So she bypassed the research-backed strategy build in lieu of fast execution. We implemented a test and pivot strategy for the company. That strategy

---

[8] Client details have been modified to respect confidentiality.
[9] The Great Resignation was an economic trend during which employees voluntarily resigned from their jobs in large scale beginning in 2021 in the wake of the COVID-19 pandemic for reasons including the rising cost of living amid wage stagnation, lack of career advancement opportunities, and inflexible telecommuting policies.

involves throwing dozens and sometimes as many as hundreds of variables against the wall to see what consumers respond to and, eventually, narrowing the focus down to the message, visual, offer, channel, and audience segmentation options that deliver most. In the end, my team estimated that it took almost seven months longer to achieve the CEO's growth goals than if we had started with reliable research. Panorama suffered an estimated $75,000 to $100,000 in marketing investment waste—indicative of the risks of the test and pivot approach. The research would have cost her $30,000 to execute over 75 days.

Sometimes, it pays to slow down to speed up.

START A REVOLUTION: CHAMPION MARKET RESEARCH AS A DO-OR-DIE INVESTMENT.

12 BATTLES™ FRAMEWORK

1 YOU **ACCEPT** THAT YOU DESERVE AND WILL ACHIEVE GUARANTEED MARKETING OUTCOMES.

2 YOU **ACKNOWLEDGE** THAT YOU DON'T REALLY KNOW THY CUSTOMER.

3 YOU **CHAMPION** MARKET RESEARCH AS A DO-OR-DIE INVESTMENT.

4 YOU **EMBRACE** THE POWER OF ATTRIBUTION MODELING AND STOP ACCEPTING BAD DATA.

5 YOU **OWN** AN OPENING IN THE BRANDSCAPE.

6 YOU **TORCH** YOUR EXISTING STRATEGY UNAPOLOGETICALLY IF NEEDED.

7 YOU **ADVOCATE** FOR AN INVESTMENT IN EACH STAGE OF THE CUSTOMER JOURNEY.

8 YOU **CHALLENGE** YOUR TEAM TO MAKE POWERFUL STRATEGIC SHIFTS GROUNDED IN RESEARCH VERSUS TRADITION.

9 YOU **PREACH** THE GOOD WORD OF DISCIPLINED OPTIMIZATION.

10 YOU **COMMIT** TO BUILDING A PAY-FOR-PERFORMANCE TEAM AROUND YOUR STRATEGY; NOT VICE VERSA.

11 YOU **REQUIRE** A POWERFUL MARKETING DASHBOARD AND DOCUMENTED PROCESSES.

12 YOU **INSPIRE** YOUR TEAM TO STAND BEHIND THEIR MROI PROJECTIONS.

BATTLE 4 : YOU **EMBRACE** THE POWER OF ATTRIBUTION MODELING AND STOP ACCEPTING BAD DATA

Battle 4

Battle 4 encourages you to embrace the power of attribution modeling and stop accepting bad data.

Calculating MROI is vital when assessing whether your investments are yielding profitable returns. This metric cuts through the noise to answer the only key question: Are you earning more than you're spending on marketing?

The Calculation

MROI = (New sales generated – Marketing costs) / Marketing costs (multiply the result by 100 to convert the dollar amount to a percent)

On the surface, calculating MROI sounds like a piece of cake. But underneath the surface, in the details, is where most organizations unknowingly overinflate this calculation, giving them a false sense of performance. As the saying goes, "Garbage in, garbage out."

Inaccurate or incomplete data can lead to misleading MROI figures, jeopardizing your strategic decisions.

> **MOST ORGANIZATIONS OVERINFLATE THEIR MROI CALCULATION, GIVING THEM A FALSE SENSE OF PERFORMANCE AND JEOPARDIZING THEIR STRATEGIC DECISIONS.**

Consider this scenario: You're evaluating the MROI of a digital campaign. Naturally, you remember the advertising spend. But it doesn't stop there. Every component contributing to the campaign must be accounted for—the cost of the time spent by your copywriter and designer, software costs, stock photography costs, and more. Only when you include every expense can you prevent your MROI from being artificially inflated.

To be even more precise, swap revenue with gross profit in your MROI calculation. While this approach will yield more conservative figures, it ensures that your marketing investments contribute positively to your bottom line. Calculating MROI based on gross profit safeguards your business against allocating resources to strategies that fail to generate enough profit to foster growth.

A Real-World Example
I'll put these concepts into practice with a real-world example from one of our clients for a large-scale Google PPC campaign.

Marketing costs

- Google digital advertising costs: $213,848

- Agency fees for advertising management: $75,000

- Lead decision maker's compensation—client side (3 percent involvement = 3 percent of salary): $2,924

- Software costs: $18,473 + $12,672 + $7,290 = $38,435

- Asset costs (stock photography): $950

- Total marketing costs: $331,157

Gains generated

This PPC campaign generated $8,977,112 in new contracts for the client. With an average gross profit margin of 55 percent, this translates to $4,937,411 in gross profit.

Now, applying the formula, calculate the MROI:

$$MROI = (\$4,937,411 - \$331,157) / \$331,157 = \$13.90 \text{ in gross}$$
$$\text{profit generated for every \$1 invested (or 1390 percent)—}$$
$$\text{approximately a \$14:\$1 MROI.}$$

CHECK OUT THE 12 BATTLES™ READER HUB at marketingtoolsforyou.com for this free resource:

MROI CALCULATOR

While it would be easy to stop your analysis here, given the strong MROI figure, the data alone doesn't provide the full picture.

Interpreting MROI

To sharpen your MROI analysis, consider whether it exceeds industry norms. A robust MROI, especially when gross profit is used, is typically 300 percent or a $3:$1 return, but to truly gauge performance, compare your MROI against your industry's specific benchmarks. In the case where you don't have access to industry-specific benchmarks, create your own by monitoring your MROI over several quarters, striving to outperform your own baseline.

CHECK OUT THE 12 BATTLES™ READER HUB at marketingtoolsforyou.com for this free resource:

INDUSTRY SPECIFIC MROI TARGETS

Next, overdeliver by looking deeper than benchmarks. An exceptionally high MROI may suggest missed opportunities for lower-margin sales. An MROI of $2:$1 is notable, whereas an extraordinary $100:$1 suggests budget constraints are hindering growth. Investigate potential gains from increased investment in the early customer journey stages. Despite higher costs for initial engagement, such as raising awareness before purchase consideration, this strategy could significantly expand your market share.

Investing in the awareness stage of the customer journey, as opposed to the consideration or conversion stages, is more costly because it involves broader targeting and more extensive outreach efforts to capture the attention of potential customers who are not yet actively looking to buy. It also requires more frequency of message than in later stages. During the awareness stage, potential customers are first introduced to your company, product, or service. This introduction can occur passively, such as when they encounter an online ad while going about their daily activities, or it can be an active process where individuals have a specific need and are in the early stages of learning about available solutions. Getting noticed in the awareness stage often requires a multi-channel approach—

leveraging advertising, content marketing, public relations, and social media—to educate and inform a diverse audience. The goal is to plant the seeds of brand recognition and preference early on so that when consumers reach the decision-making or consideration stage, they are already familiar with the brand and trust it. This foundational work is resource-intensive but will lead to a commanding presence in the market and a larger share of future sales.

Takeaway: A higher MROI isn't always indicative of optimal marketing plan performance.

A HIGHER MROI ISN'T ALWAYS INDICATIVE OF OPTIMAL MARKETING PLAN PERFORMANCE.

With clarity regarding the overall returns your marketing plan is delivering, let's have a look at the performance of your individual marketing tactics.

Attribution Modeling

What Is Attribution Modeling?

While it's relatively straightforward to measure the overall impact of your marketing efforts, it's decidedly trickier to determine which marketing channel or touchpoint should get the credit for a new sale. Too few middle-market companies do this effectively, leading to sizable marketing waste.

Enter attribution modeling—a powerful tool that reveals the intricate matrix of customer interactions with your brand as well as which of those interactions is actually driving prospective customer behavior. Attribution modeling is the process of assigning credit to different marketing touchpoints that influence the customer journey toward conversion. Simply put, it helps businesses understand which marketing channels, campaigns, or interactions play a role in driving a customer to make a purchase or take a desired action and to what degree. This is especially important at a time when customers engage with a brand through multiple touchpoints—eight on average—before deciding to purchase.

Imagine a B2B company that runs digital advertising, social media campaigns, email marketing, and hosts webinars. A potential customer might first come across the company's ad on a search engine, then visit its website. They may then subscribe to its newsletter after clicking on a social media post. And then, after attending a webinar that they learned about through email, they decide to make a purchase. Attribution modeling helps decode this complex journey and answer critical questions such as:

- Which marketing channel had the most significant impact on the final decision?

- How do different touchpoints contribute to revenue generation?

- How can marketing budgets be optimized based on the most effective channels?

- What kind of impact would reduction of investment in any one touchpoint have on conversion rates?

Why Attribution Modeling Matters

Attribution modeling is not just a trendy concept; it is a fundamental aspect of modern marketing strategy. Here's why it matters, particularly for middle-market CEOs and marketing leaders.

Data-driven decision making: Attribution modeling provides data-backed insights, allowing leaders to make informed decisions on where to allocate precious marketing resources for the best ROI based on the marketing touchpoints truly responsible for converting a prospect to a customer rather than only the last touchpoint prior to a sale, which is all too common.

Resource optimization: By identifying high-impact marketing channels, businesses can allocate their budgets more effectively and avoid wasteful spending on less productive channels.

Customer journey understanding: Attribution modeling helps companies better understand the customer journey, enabling them to tailor marketing messaging to specific touchpoints based on what information customers need at that point in their buying journey.

Improved MROI: When leaders have a clear view of what's driving actual conversions, they can fine-tune their strategies to maximize MROI, which is especially crucial for companies with limited resources.

Attribution modeling is like golfing with a caddy who knows every inch of the course. You might have a good swing, but without your caddy's insights on where to aim and which club to use, you're just as likely to end up in the sand trap as on the green. Attribution modeling tells you where your marketing strokes are landing, turning guesswork into a game of skill. It's the difference between swinging blindly and aiming for a hole-in-one with every shot.

> **WITH A CLEAR VIEW OF WHAT'S DRIVING ACTUAL CONVERSIONS, YOU CAN FINE-TUNE YOUR STRATEGIES TO MAXIMIZE MROI, WHICH IS ESPECIALLY CRUCIAL FOR COMPANIES WITH LIMITED RESOURCES.**

Types of Attribution Modeling

There are various attribution models, each with its own set of rules for distributing credit to different touchpoints along the customer journey. In order to review the most common models, I'll use the following customer journey as a frame of reference throughout this section.

In this sample (the image that follows), this company's average customer journey from first interaction with the company to becoming a customer has eight steps. Step 1 is the customer's Google search (also called an organic search as opposed to a paid search where the customer clicks on a paid Google Ad). Steps 2 through 7 see the customer engage with a blog, a Google Ad, two drip emails, a promotional video on the website, and a retargeting ad that delivers branded ads to the customer after they leave the website. The final step is a direct visit to the company's website where the customer makes a purchase.

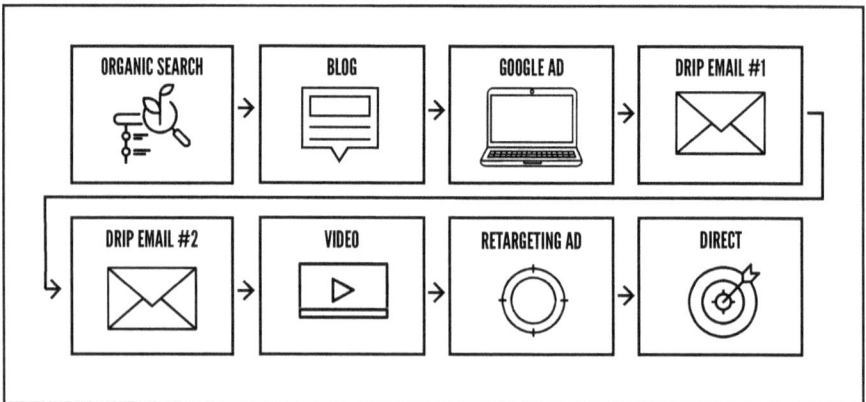

I'll apply the most common attribution models to this customer journey and assess the impact.

First-touch attribution: In this model, all credit for a conversion is assigned to the first touchpoint a customer interacts with. Here, the credit goes to the customer's organic Google search. It's a straightforward approach but can be overly simplistic, as it ignores the contribution of subsequent interactions.

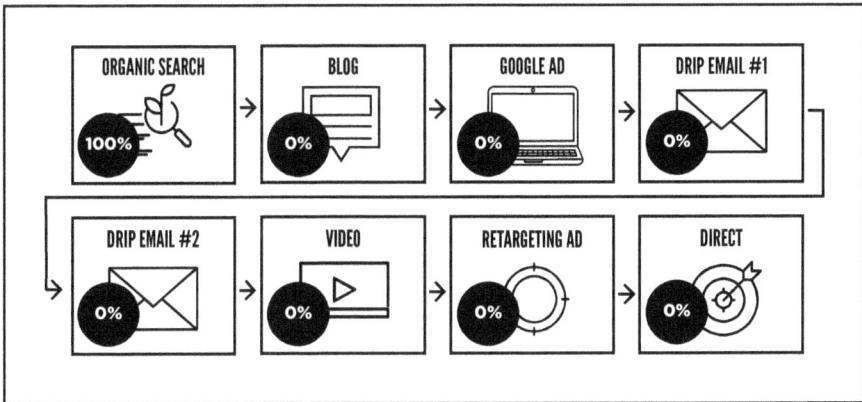

- **Pros:** This model is easy to implement and provides a clear starting point.

- **Cons:** It ignores the impact of other touchpoints on the conversion journey.

- **Ideal for:** B2B companies with relatively short and straight-forward sales cycles where the initial interaction plays a decisive role in conversion. This model suits industries where customers make quick purchasing decisions based on immediate needs or familiarity with the brand.

- **Examples:** SaaS companies with short sales cycles that offer free trials, e-commerce businesses with one-time purchase products, and event management services with quick-turn ticket purchases.

Last-touch attribution: This model gives all the credit for a conversion to the final touchpoint before that conversion. Here, the credit goes to the direct visit to the website. This model is the most common default attribution model used by most marketing automation platforms. While it acknowledges the last interaction, it neglects the roles of preceding touchpoints.

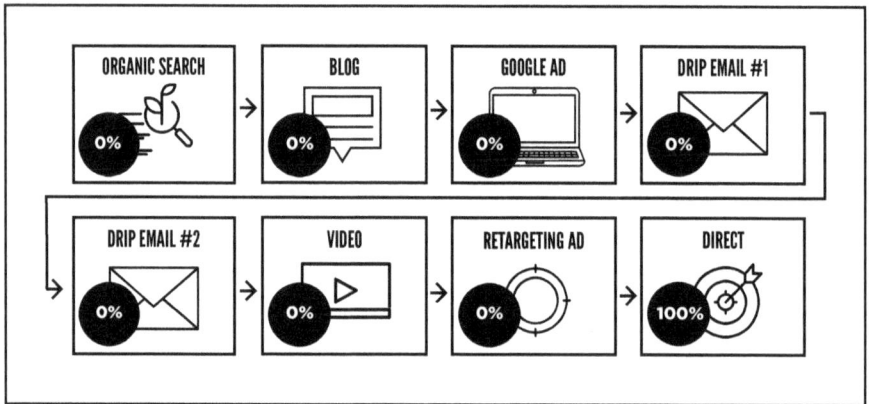

- **Pros:** This model is simple to implement and highlights the immediate pre-conversion touchpoint.

- **Cons:** It fails to recognize the influence of earlier interactions.

- **Ideal for:** B2B companies with well-defined conversion points that occur shortly after the final interaction. This model works for industries where the last touchpoint is often the most critical (i.e., where a consultation or proposal submission makes or breaks the sale).

- **Examples:** Businesses offering consulting, legal, or financial services.

Linear attribution: In this model, credit is distributed equally among all touchpoints in the customer journey. Here, all eight touchpoints earn equal credit for a sale. This approach offers a more balanced view of each touchpoint's contribution.

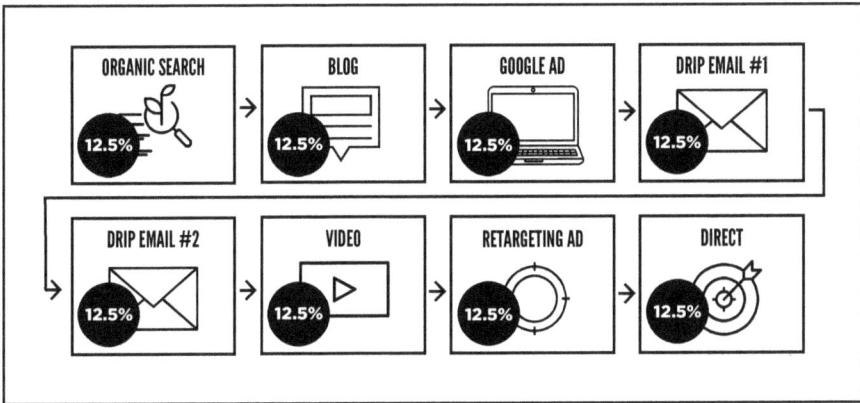

- **Pros:** This model distributes credit evenly across all touchpoints and acknowledges the role of each.

- **Cons:** It may not accurately represent the actual impact of certain touchpoints.

- **Ideal for:** B2B companies operating in industries with complex sales cycles. This model is suitable when various marketing efforts contribute significantly at different stages of the customer journey.

- **Examples:** Industrial equipment manufacturers, enterprise software providers, and supply-chain logistics companies.

Time-decay attribution: This model gives more credit to touchpoints that are closer to the conversion event while gradually reducing the credit assigned to earlier interactions. It recognizes that interactions closer to conversion often have a more significant impact. Here, the direct visit to the website earns the most credit while each preceding touchpoint earns less credit than the touchpoint after it. While the breakdown of the weighting will vary by company, the following image illustrates the principle. Note that with time decay, there are usually more high-impact touchpoints toward the end of the customer journey, such as a webinar or proposal delivery.

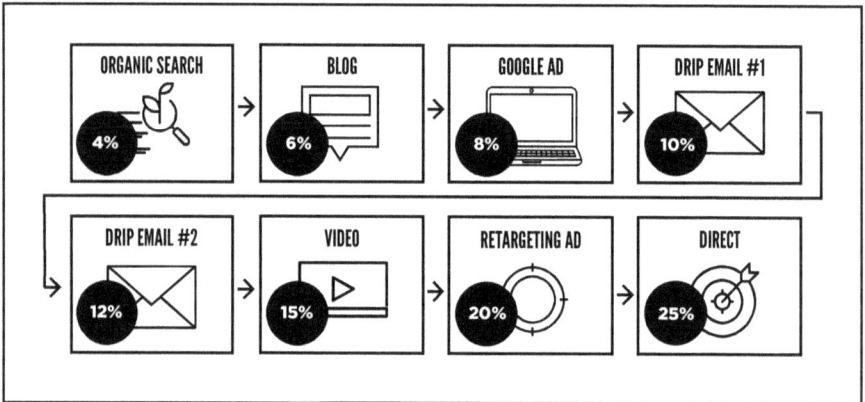

- **Pros:** This model reflects the importance of touchpoints closer to conversion.

- **Cons:** It still doesn't fully capture the nuanced impact of each touchpoint.

- **Ideal for:** B2B companies with long and intricate sales cycles where early nurturing and education are essential but the significance of touchpoints increases as the prospect approaches conversion. This model suits industries where customer relationships are built over time.

- **Examples:** Healthcare technology providers, financial services firms, and business-consulting companies.

Data-driven attribution: This Google Analytics attribution model doesn't use predefined weighting to assign credit to each touchpoint. Instead, it uses machine learning to create a custom model for the company by collecting the actual data that reflects its customers' journeys through the touchpoints including paid search, social media campaigns, etc. It also takes into account user interactions with the company's website, such as the length of time for conversion, device type, creative asset type, and number and order of ad interactions. Note that this model requires sufficient historical data in order to provide reliable insights, so for a company just beginning to use Google Analytics or with low traffic volumes, the data won't be reliable or as effective.

- **Pros:** This model is automatically tailored to a company's needs and analyzes a wide range of elements. It removes bias and guesswork, as it's based on actual data. It also distributes credit across a variety of touchpoints, as with linear and time-decay attribution, versus giving sole credit to a single touchpoint like in last- or first-touch attribution.

- **Cons:** The specific calculations are not disclosed, which requires a company to trust in the system's accuracy without transparency. Moreover, this model is limited to advertising touchpoints that Google Analytics can access, potentially missing, for example, email campaigns if the email platform isn't connected to Google Analytics.

- **Ideal for:** B2B companies that have complex buying cycles with multiple channels and touchpoints, as well as substantial customer interaction data.

- **Examples:** Insurance, engineering, construction, education, and corporate training.

Custom attribution models: Many businesses develop their own attribution models that are tailored to their unique customer journey and business goals. These models can incorporate data from multiple touchpoints and assign credit based on specific criteria— meaning weights are customized for each touchpoint based on the nuances of the customer journey in that specific industry.

- **Pros:** This model is highly customizable and reflects the intricacies of the business.

- **Cons:** It may require more data and expertise for effective implementation.

- **Ideal for:** B2B companies with unique customer journeys that don't fit neatly into standardized attribution models. Custom models are suitable when specific criteria such as lead scoring, industry benchmarks, or engagement levels hold particular importance in determining attribution:

  - Lead scoring may spur a company to develop a custom attribution model because it can attribute more credit to touchpoints that engage higher-value leads.

  - Industry benchmarks can drive development of a custom attribution model by providing external reference points for assigning weight to different touchpoints, ensuring the model aligns with broader market trends and performance standards.

  - Engagement levels may support the creation of a custom attribution model by offering insights into how different interactions affect the customer journey, enabling the model to assign more credit to touchpoints that drive higher engagement and ultimately lead to conversions.

- **Examples:** High-tech manufacturers with highly segmented target markets, niche B2B service providers, and companies with diverse product portfolios.

Now that you understand the most common types of attribution models, let's explore attribution model measurement, determine which models are the best fit for your company, and identify what actions to take according to your data.

A Practical Example

To better understand how attribution platforms calculate CAC based on various attribution models, let's look at an example.

First, note the formula for determining CAC in the context of attribution modeling:

Marketing costs for a given touchpoint / Number of conversions attributed to that touchpoint

Assume a company runs a single marketing campaign that includes paid search, social media, email, and retargeting display ads, and assume the typical customer journey is in that order. The company spends a total of $10,000 and generates $80,000 in revenue from 80 new customers at a transaction size of $1,000 per new customer. Broken down, the $10,000 expense looks like this: $5,000 in paid search, $2,000 in social media ads, $1,000 in email marketing, and $2,000 in retargeting display ads.

The company then applies two different attribution models—first-touch and linear—to this campaign:

First-touch attribution model results: All the credit is given to the touchpoint first touched by the customer prior to purchase.

- Paid search: Assume that 60 conversions (or new customers) valued at $1,000 each get attributed to this touchpoint because it was the first interaction before these new customers made a purchase making the revenue attributed to this touchpoint $60,000. With $5,000 in ad spend, the CAC = $83.33. Here's the math:

$$CAC = \frac{\text{Total spend on paid search}}{\text{Conversions attributed to paid search}}$$

$$CAC = \frac{\$5,000}{60} = \$83.33$$

- Social media: 10 conversions attributed to this touchpoint or $10,000 in revenue, $2,000 in ad spend, CAC = $200

- Email marketing: 5 conversions attributed to this touchpoint or $5,000 in revenue, $1,000 in ad spend, CAC = $200

- Retargeting display ads: 5 conversions attributed to this touchpoint or $5,000 in revenue, $2,000 in ad spend, CAC = $400

Linear attribution model results: Every touchpoint in a customer journey leading to a conversion is given equal credit. If a customer journey had four touchpoints—paid search, social media, email, and retargeting display ads—each would receive 25 percent credit for that conversion assuming customers convert after the fourth touchpoint. If they convert after the second touchpoint, which is through social media, then paid search and social media would each earn 50 percent credit for that conversion. Assuming 80 new customers that all convert after the fourth touchpoint, for simplicity's sake, the linear model would attribute 20 of these new customers and 25 percent of the revenue to each of the marketing touchpoints deployed. Consider the following example that uses the same assumptions regarding budget breakdown across channels and the average transaction size of $1,000.

- Paid search: 20 conversions attributed to this touchpoint or $20,000 in revenue. With $5,000 in paid search ad spend, the CAC = $250. Here's the math:

$$CAC = \frac{\text{Total spend on paid search}}{\text{Conversions attributed to paid search}}$$

$$CAC = \frac{\$5,000}{20} = \$250$$

- Social media: 20 conversions attributed to this touchpoint or $20,000 in revenue, $2,000 in ad spend, CAC = $100

- Email marketing: 20 conversions attributed to this touchpoint or $20,000 in revenue, $1,000 in ad spend, CAC = $50

- Retargeting display ads: 20 conversions attributed to this touchpoint or $20,000 in revenue, $2,000 in ad spend, CAC = $100

CHECK OUT THE 12 BATTLES™ READER HUB at marketingtoolsforyou.com for this free resource:

ATTRIBUTION MODEL ASSESSMENT

Analysis
- The first-touch attribution model gives full credit to the first touchpoint before the conversion, which can favor a channel like

paid search if customers typically engage with paid search ads toward the start of their customer journey. The first-touch case study indicates that the CAC is lower with paid search than with any of the other touchpoints.

- The linear model, however, spreads the credit for each conversion equally across all the touchpoints that contributed to the conversion regardless of their position in the conversion path. This model gives email marketing the advantage due to its relatively low cost to deploy.

Determination

- By looking at the linear model, the company realizes that channels previously undervalued, such as email marketing, social media ads, and retargeting display ads, play a significant role in the conversion process. Conversely, when it looks at paid search, the first-touch model might drive it to invest more due to the low CAC or invest less based on the high CAC in the linear model.

- The overall revenue and total conversions remain the same, but the distribution of credit across channels changes. This can lead to a more strategic allocation of the marketing budget in future campaigns. If the analysis reveals that the first-touch model is the most accurate representation of the customers' buying experience, then heavying up the paid search investment makes sense. If the linear model seems best aligned with the customers' reality, then a larger investment in email marketing is logical.

In this example, both attribution models assess the exact same campaign data; the difference lies in the way the credit for conversions is distributed, which can significantly influence the perceived performance of each marketing channel and the strategic decisions that follow.

Identifying the Ideal Attribution Model

Objectively determining the most accurate attribution model for your business is challenging because accuracy in this context is less about precision and more about which model aligns best with your understanding of your customers' behaviors and your marketing objectives. However, there are several steps you can take to make a more informed decision.

Qualitative feedback: Collect qualitative feedback from customers about their customer journey. Surveys or interviews can provide insights into which touchpoints they recall or felt were influential in their decision-making processes. This is one of the most effective ways to validate that you have selected the appropriate attribution model.

A/B testing: Run controlled experiments where different attribution models are used to inform the marketing spend, then compare the outcomes. If increasing the spend of a touchpoint that you thought was a major contributor to conversion doesn't move the needle, then you know your attribution model is flawed. These experiments involve segmenting your audience into comparable groups, allocating marketing budgets based on different attribution models, closely measuring KPIs, and comparing results. When you allocate your marketing budget based on differing attribution models, you would distribute your budget differently for each group:

- For the group testing first-touch attribution, you'd allocate more budget to the initial touchpoint that introduces customers to your brand, like paid search in the prior example.

- In the last-touch attribution group, you'd allocate more budget to the touchpoint just before conversion, like retargeting campaigns from that example.

By conducting these structured experiments, you can gain powerful insights into your ideal attribution model.

> **QUALITATIVE FEEDBACK FROM CUSTOMERS ABOUT THEIR JOURNEY AND A/B TESTING ARE TWO OF THE MOST EFFECTIVE WAYS TO VALIDATE YOUR ATTRIBUTION MODEL SELECTION.**

Historical data analysis: Examine past campaigns with the different models applied. Which model's results make the most sense when compared to known customer behaviors and outcomes?

Predictive validation: Use the models to predict the outcome of future marketing efforts based on historical data, then measure the actual outcomes against those predictions to see which model was closer to reality.

Correlation with sales data: Cross reference the attribution data with sales and CRM data. Does one model correlate better with the sales funnel progression or LTV? This process allows you to see if the touchpoints deemed important by the chosen attribution model genuinely lead to higher sales or improved customer loyalty. For instance, if a model emphasizes the importance of a particular digital ad in driving conversions, correlating this with sales data can validate whether customers who interacted with that ad made higher value purchases. Similarly, examining LTV in relation to the touchpoints identified can reveal if those interactions are associated with more valuable, long-term customers.

Expert consultation: Work with data analysts or marketing attribution experts to review the models' outcomes. Their experience can help identify which model seems most reasonable.

Consistency with industry standards: Consider which models are being used by peer groups in the industry and whether those models are reported to work well for them.

Customer journey complexity: Consider the length and complexity of the customer journey. More complex journeys may require more sophisticated multi-touch models. For instance, in a B2B software industry where the decision-making process involves multiple stakeholders and a lengthy evaluation period, a linear attribution model that evenly distributes credit to all touchpoints may provide a more accurate representation of how each interaction contributes to the final conversion. In contrast, a simple, short consumer journey for a low-cost online product might be adequately captured by a first-touch attribution model.

Ultimately, the most accurate model is one that reliably informs strategy and improves marketing performance. It's important to recognize that attribution modeling is not an exact science but a tool to guide strategic decisions, and one attribution model may need to be customized to fit the unique aspects of a business based on your industry, sales cycle, and customer behavior. Keep in mind that the ideal attribution model may evolve as a B2B company's marketing strategy, customer behavior, and industry landscape change. Regularly reviewing and adjusting the chosen model to align with business goals is a best practice.

Taking Action Based on Attribution Model Results

Once you've landed on an ideal attribution model, it's time to act on the data presented. Here's a list of the top 10 next steps to consider:

1. **Allocate budget more effectively:** Use the data to identify which channels are most effective at driving conversions, and allocate more budget to these areas. Conversely, reduce spending on channels that are underperforming, and continuously monitor their performance.

2. **Refine marketing tactics:** Assess stages in the customer journey where certain channels have the most impact. Tailor the content and tactics on these channels to better engage the target audience at specific stages. For instance, if your attribution data shows that email marketing plays a crucial role in the consideration stage, optimize your email campaigns to provide more informative content and personalized offers to potential customers in that stage.

3. **Improve customer targeting:** Use insights from the attribution model to understand the characteristics and behaviors of your most valuable customers. Refine your targeting criteria by applying these insights to future campaigns. You might target your ads more precisely to the demographic that converts most often or design your email content to appeal more to the preferences shown by your best customers. The goal is to focus your marketing resources on the people who are most likely to bring value to your business, making each campaign more effective and efficient.

4. **Test and optimize:** Continuously test different aspects of your marketing campaigns (such as ad copy, design, targeting, etc.) based on the insights from the attribution model. Use A/B testing to validate any changes and optimize your marketing campaigns for better performance. An attribution model, for example, might indicate that emails highlighting product features and the benefits of those features lead to conversions. To test this, create two email versions: one with your usual content and another with highly-emphasized product features. Send these to similar audiences and compare conversion rates to see if heavily emphasizing features drives more conversions.

5. **Enhance cross-channel harmony:** Identify how different channels influence each other, and optimize each channel for cross-channel marketing. Ensure that messaging and branding

are consistent across channels for a cohesive customer experience. If an attribution model shows, for example, that customers often engage with a social media post before signing up for a newsletter and then make a purchase after receiving an email promotion, this indicates a journey across channels with each step contributing to the conversion. To enhance cross-channel harmony, ensure consistency across social media posts and emails by utilizing a design theme that incorporates consistent color schemes, fonts, and visual elements to reinforce brand identity and deliver a seamless customer experience. Use social media to tease upcoming email promotions, creating anticipation. And align email content with the most engaging social media posts to reinforce the message. The idea is to create a seamless brand experience that guides customers naturally from one channel to the next, increasing the likelihood of conversion.

6. **Monitor and adapt:** Regularly review the performance data provided by the attribution model. Be prepared to adapt strategies as market conditions, consumer behaviors, and technologies evolve.

7. **Integrate with other data:** Combine insights from the attribution model with other business data, such as sales, customer service interactions, and market trends, to gain a more comprehensive view of your business' marketing performance.

8. **Communicate findings and educate teams:** Share the insights from the attribution model with all relevant teams (sales, customer service, product development, etc.) to ensure everyone understands how their work contributes to the overall business goals. Educate them on the importance of the chosen attribution model in decision making.

9. **Set realistic KPIs:** Based on the insights from the attribution model, set realistic and measurable KPIs for future campaigns.

For example, if the attribution model indicates that social media impacts early-stage customer engagement, set KPIs around engagement metrics such as shares and comments rather than just conversion rates. This approach ensures that your KPIs are aligned with the actual leading indicators of new business outcomes as revealed by your attribution analysis.

10. **Leverage technology:** Utilize marketing technology tools and platforms that can integrate with your attribution model for automated data collection, analysis, and reporting. For example, use Google Analytics combined with a CRM such as Salesforce. Google Analytics tracks user behavior across your website and digital campaigns, attributing actions such as page visits, form submissions, and e-commerce transactions to various marketing efforts. Most importantly, Google Analytics allows you to select the most appropriate attribution model for your company. This data can feed into Salesforce, which then records which interactions lead to conversions. Note that Google Analytics doesn't allow for as many attribution model types as other platforms like HubSpot.

By taking these actions, your business can make data-driven decisions that enhance the effectiveness of its marketing efforts, ultimately leading to improved MROI and business growth. Executing a marketing plan without attribution modeling is like going into battle without intelligence. You can engage the enemy with all your manpower, but without knowing where your efforts are most effective, much of your firepower could be wasted on the wrong targets. Attribution modeling acts like a recon team by giving you critical insights into where your strategies are hitting the mark, allowing you to deploy your resources with tactical precision.

CHECK OUT THE 12 BATTLES™ READER HUB at marketingtoolsforyou.com for this free resource:

ATTRIBUTION MODELING PLATFORMS

Battle 4 Research Insights[10]

23% of middle-market B2B companies earn a $3:$1 or $4:$1 MROI, making it the most common MROI range realized among survey respondents. MROI performance improves as the size of the marketing investment increases. How does your company stack up? Are you getting a complete picture of MROI? Bear in mind that most companies fail to include marketing team compensation in their MROI calculations. They also generally use revenue versus gross profit in their calculations. So these numbers might be inflated if you take a purist position on the formula.

57% of total respondents indicate their marketing team leverages attribution modeling, with the most common reasons this measurement strategy isn't used being "don't believe we need it" and "haven't heard of it." Comparatively, fewer companies using an internal team only (no agency partnership) leverage attribution modeling at just 46 percent. In the B2B space, I would argue that no company with over $2M in revenue can do without it.

Success Story

Prosperity Financial Group[11], an $8M start-up in the financial services space, had invested significantly in its marketing to rapidly

---

[10] From the "2024 RedRover U.S. Middle-Market B2B Marketing Performance Study," available in the 12 Battles™ Reader Hub at marketingtoolsforyou.com.
[11] Client details have been modified to respect confidentiality.

grow market share—to the tune of over $150,000 the last fiscal year. In our first conversation, we learned that the CEO was receiving reports indicating that marketing was paying off, but deep down she didn't trust the data—and rightfully so.

As we dug a little deeper, we learned that Google Analytics wasn't set up properly on the main U.S.-based website, and its sister company in the U.K. had Google Tag Manager set up so that conversions from its site fed into the site of the parent company—giving the parent company a false sense of success. Furthermore, the Google Ads campaign not only was placing higher bids on the U.K. company's keywords (meaning they were bidding against one another) but was also set up under a last-touch attribution model, which meant Prosperity wasn't getting the full picture of performance from critical earlier touchpoints. Given its long, complex sales cycle, a linear or data-driven attribution model would have been more effective.

As a result of this inaccurate and incomplete data, the company was pouring good money into a marketing strategy that had an extremely high CAC. To its credit, this was not a company that hesitated to pivot when needed. In fact, it had changed the primary CTA (call to action) on its website 10 times during the prior 18 months. However, without proper attribution modeling, company leadership had no idea what improvements, if any, those changes generated.

When presented with this evaluation, the CEO eagerly embraced the idea that attribution modeling—combined with the proper set up of Google Analytics and Google Tag Manager—was the path to better, actionable, and consistently reliable data. A few months into execution, the company's cost per lead had already been reduced by 53 percent.

Cautionary Tale

Fortress Texas[12], a $20M commercial and residential security services company in Dallas, Texas, was a franchisee of parent company Fortress Facility Services. This franchisee paid marketing royalties to the corporate office for the benefits gained from enterprise marketing. Still, due to the size of his operation, the president of the Dallas franchise, Mike, was looking for more individualized support from a marketing agency partner. He approached us with a desire to improve the performance of his Google PPC campaigns. He was frustrated that he was getting too many residential leads from the campaigns; in his world, residential business came at a lower margin than commercial. His request was to eliminate all residential keywords from this PPC campaign and focus 100 percent on commercial keyword combinations. On the surface, it seemed like a logical request. When we looked under the hood and dove into his analytics, however, a different story unfolded.

Mike wanted to see us cut broad keyword combinations such as "security services near me" and "security companies near me" in favor of clearly commercial combinations such as "commercial security" or "warehouse security." He knew that he was getting more residential leads than he wanted, but he didn't have the full picture on the source of those leads. In the end, after we set up proper attribution modeling, the analytics demonstrated that 75 percent of his inbound residential leads were not coming from the PPC campaign. The broad "security services/companies" keyword combinations that he wanted to kill in fact generated a full 50 percent of his commercial lead volume. The market doesn't always search for products and services in the ways you think it might. The data cuts through the noise and delivers the true picture.

In the end, there were certainly keyword combinations that were generating more residential leads than we wanted, and they were

___
[12] Client details have been modified to respect confidentiality.

cut. But there were a number of believed-to-be-residential keyword combinations that, had they been paused, would have cut his commercial lead volume in half. It took some time and some deep data insights before Mike was convinced that his instincts weren't entirely on the mark. The result was a 42 percent increase in qualified commercial leads the year after the campaigns were optimized.

> **START A REVOLUTION: EMBRACE THE POWER OF ATTRIBUTION MODELING AND STOP ACCEPTING BAD DATA.**

12 BATTLES™ FRAMEWORK

1. YOU **ACCEPT** THAT YOU DESERVE AND WILL ACHIEVE GUARANTEED MARKETING OUTCOMES.

2. YOU **ACKNOWLEDGE** THAT YOU DON'T REALLY KNOW THY CUSTOMER.

3. YOU **CHAMPION** MARKET RESEARCH AS A DO-OR-DIE INVESTMENT.

4. YOU **EMBRACE** THE POWER OF ATTRIBUTION MODELING AND STOP ACCEPTING BAD DATA.

5. YOU **OWN** AN OPENING IN THE BRANDSCAPE.

6. YOU **TORCH** YOUR EXISTING STRATEGY UNAPOLOGETICALLY IF NEEDED.

7. YOU **ADVOCATE** FOR AN INVESTMENT IN EACH STAGE OF THE CUSTOMER JOURNEY.

8. YOU **CHALLENGE** YOUR TEAM TO MAKE POWERFUL STRATEGIC SHIFTS GROUNDED IN RESEARCH VERSUS TRADITION.

9. YOU **PREACH** THE GOOD WORD OF DISCIPLINED OPTIMIZATION.

10. YOU **COMMIT** TO BUILDING A PAY-FOR-PERFORMANCE TEAM AROUND YOUR STRATEGY; NOT VICE VERSA.

11. YOU **REQUIRE** A POWERFUL MARKETING DASHBOARD AND DOCUMENTED PROCESSES.

12. YOU **INSPIRE** YOUR TEAM TO STAND BEHIND THEIR MROI PROJECTIONS.

BATTLE 5 : YOU **OWN** AN OPENING IN THE BRANDSCAPE

Battle 5

Battle 5 challenges you to own an opening in the brandscape.

The term "brandscape" isn't just a fancy buzzword; it's a crucial concept that defines your brand's position in the ever-changing marketplace. Your brandscape—derived from the words brand and landscape—is a map of your brand's territory in the online and offline world. Every brand aims not only to exist but to stand out in this vast brandscape. The question is: How can your brand go beyond simply being present to making a noteworthy impact?

Understanding the Brandscape

Before diving deep into the strategy, it's essential to grasp the essence of the "brandscape." Imagine a vast canvas painted with a myriad of colors, each representing a brand. Some colors overlap, some are bright and eye-catching, and others fade into the background. This canvas is the market, and the brandscape analysis is the keen-eyed artist who can distinguish between each hue, shade, and tint.

Your brandscape analysis must be thorough and precise. It isn't about merely identifying what differentiators competitors are staking a claim to; it's about understanding the undercurrents, the shifts, and the voids.

The Power of Differentiation

In a sea of similarities, differentiation is power. Companies that simply echo the sentiments and differentiators of others often fade into brand irrelevance. But those that dare to be different, that identify and embrace a unique position, rise above the noise.

COMPANIES THAT SIMPLY ECHO THE SENTIMENTS AND DIFFERENTIATORS OF OTHERS OFTEN FADE INTO BRAND IRRELEVANCE. BUT THOSE THAT DARE TO BE DIFFERENT, THAT IDENTIFY AND EMBRACE A UNIQUE POSITION, RISE ABOVE THE NOISE.

For the CEO or marketing leader, understanding this is not just essential, it's transformative. A business' success hinges on its ability to stand out, to be recognized, and to be remembered. By seeking out and claiming an open space in the brandscape, companies not only distinguish themselves but also secure a vantage point from which they can better address their target market.

Conducting a Brandscape Analysis

A brandscape analysis is an evaluation of the overall environment in which a brand operates. It offers actionable insights that drive informed decision making. Follow these five steps when conducting a brandscape analysis:

1. **Identify key players:** Begin by listing your biggest competitors. This list should come from a combination of your stakeholder interviews and your customer surveys. It's important to assess both who your internal team and your customers believe you

compete against. This isn't just about the big names, but also about the niche players who might be claiming a significant space in the brandscape.

2. **Pinpoint decision-making criteria:** Pinpoint the differentiators most crucial to your potential customers. These are the factors that sway decisions, shape opinions, and drive purchases. To choose the top two decision-making factors that truly inspire a prospective customer to buy in your industry, leverage your research—specifically your customer survey.

3. **Plot the brandscape:** A brandscape is a grid with X and Y axes that allows you to compare how your brand positioning stacks up against that of your top competitors on two important customer decision-making criteria. Use the X axis to measure one of those decision-making criteria and the Y axis to measure the other. At the end of each axis, note the range of brand positioning that you and your competitors communicate for that particular decision-making criteria—from the best offering in the market to the worst. Now, plot each of your top competitors on the brandscape based on where their positioning places them. This gives you a graphical representation of where each brand stands. Note: If there are more than two critical customer decision-making criteria to consider, you will need multiple brandscape graphs.

In the following simple brandscape grid example, you'll see an opening in the market. The lower left quadrant of the grid is completely unoccupied, giving the company in this example, a commercial HVAC supply house, an opportunity to make a strategic shift in positioning and service offering and create a truly unique value proposition as a result. Today, the company provides free standard same-day shipping. If it improves its offering to free expedited shipping while still maintaining same-day shipping, it will own a unique position in the brandscape.

BRANDSCAPE

SHIPS WITHIN 3 BUSINESS DAYS

Competitor A   Competitor B

EXPEDITED SHIPPING FREE ←————————————→ STANDARD SHIPPING FREE

Competitor C

You - Today

SHIPS SAME DAY

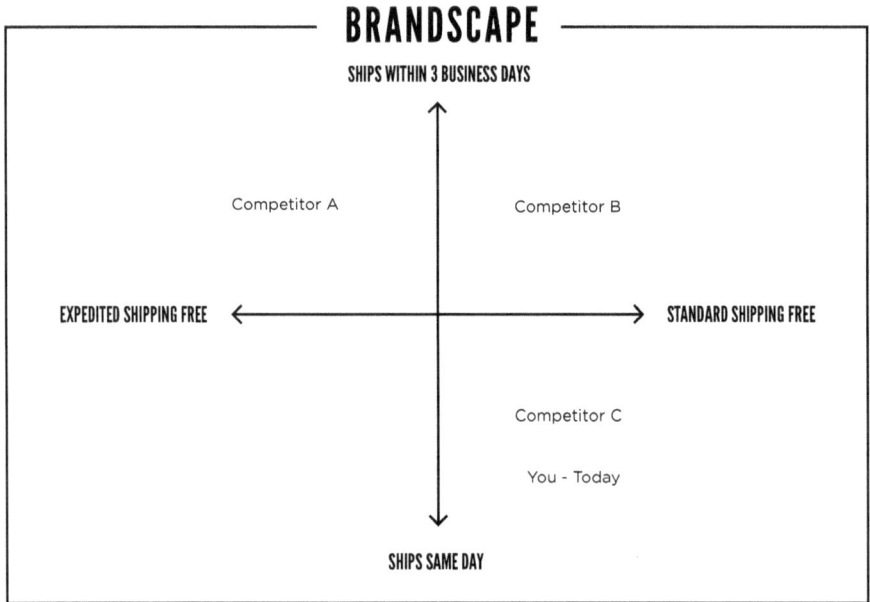

If your company is a professional services firm, you might evaluate industry specialization with the willingness to be accessible after hours. If you're Nike, your brandscape might be far less tangible—including visual storytelling and aspirational messaging.

4. **Seek out the gaps:** Once you have the brandscape laid out, it becomes easier to spot the gaps. These are the unclaimed areas teeming with untouched opportunities. Naturally, not every gap is an opportunity. In the brandscape example, even if Competitor B wasn't in the picture, it wouldn't make sense to own the "standard shipping within three business days" quadrant (upper right) simply because it is available because Competitors A and C have stronger offers.

5. **Reposition if necessary:** If a gap you identify in the market is viable and aligns with your brand's core values and mission, consider repositioning. Adjusting your brand messaging to fill this void can give you an unparalleled advantage because you are

taking ownership of a unique value proposition that is important to your targeted customers and not claimed by others. Keep in mind that if it's a positioning adjustment that may be easy for your competitors to replicate, you'd better flood the market with your new messaging so you can steal as much share as possible before they catch up. Speed to market wins here.

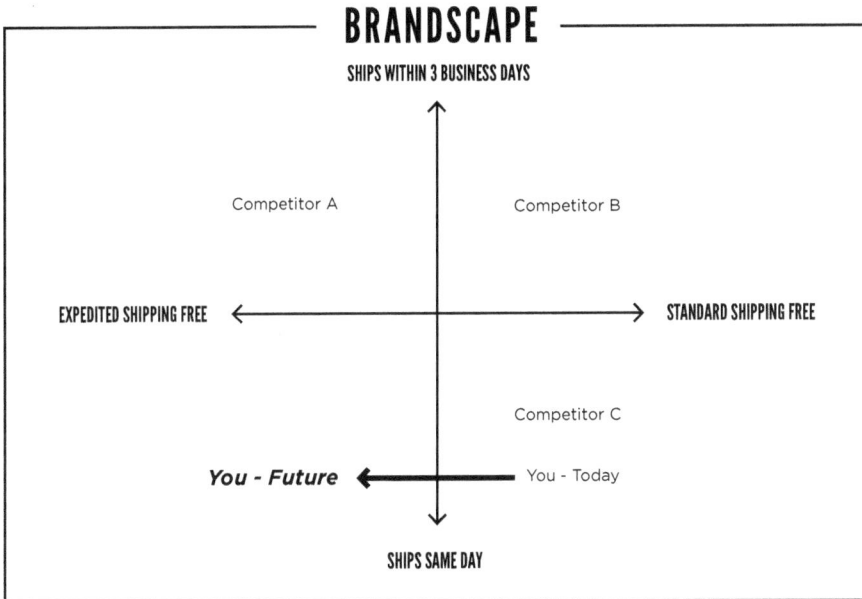

BRANDSCAPE

SHIPS WITHIN 3 BUSINESS DAYS

Competitor A   Competitor B

EXPEDITED SHIPPING FREE ←————————————————→ STANDARD SHIPPING FREE

Competitor C

You - Future ←————— You - Today

SHIPS SAME DAY

Embracing Your Position

Once you've identified your unique position in the brandscape, embrace it wholeheartedly. It's a commitment—a declaration that you are here to fill a void, to offer something that others aren't. It's a chance to claim a space that is uniquely yours—a space that resonates with your brand's values and vision and, most importantly, the market!

Moreover, finding and embracing your position often leads to further innovation. When brands realize that they can claim a particular space in the market, they are driven to innovate to solidify their position. This drive leads to groundbreaking products, services, and solutions.

Thus, a new brandscape position (based on a thorough brandscape analysis) doesn't just benefit the marketing department; it also fuels the research and development, product development, and customer service teams, catalyzing creativity.

This revolution in mindset to own a position in the brandscape challenges businesses to introspect, re-evaluate their strategies, and dare to be different. And in this challenge lies the promise of a unique position in a crowded marketplace and the promise of a voice that is not just heard but also remembered.

> **IN YOUR BRANDSCAPE LIES THE PROMISE OF A UNIQUE POSITION IN A CROWDED MARKETPLACE AND THE PROMISE OF A VOICE THAT IS NOT JUST HEARD BUT ALSO REMEMBERED.**

The Domino Effect

But beware: Once a brand repositions itself to fill a gap in the brandscape, it often triggers a domino effect. Competitors take notice, markets shift, and new trends emerge. As a CEO or marketing leader, it's essential to not only be aware of this but to anticipate it. The brandscape is dynamic, and today's clear opening might be tomorrow's crowded space. Continuous analysis, agility, and adaptability are the keys to ensuring that a brand remains relevant and dominant. Given its importance, businesses should conduct a brandscape analysis quarterly to adapt to market changes, competitor movements, and emerging trends.

Case Studies: Brands That Owned Their Space

In marketing, revolution is not just about breaking the mold; it's about creating a new one. And in the brandscape, your brand doesn't just belong; it owns. Own your space, embrace your position, and let the world see the unique hue that is your brand.

Consider brands like Salesforce, Microsoft LinkedIn, and Slack. While they operate in different subspecialties of the technology sector, these B2B giants have each identified a gap in their respective markets and positioned themselves as distinct leaders in the field. Their success stories are not solely about innovative products or services; they're also about carving out a unique position in a crowded marketplace.

Salesforce: Salesforce revolutionized the CRM industry by not only providing a cloud-based CRM platform but also by creating an ecosystem of integrated applications. It positioned itself as an innovator in cloud computing, transforming how businesses interact with their customers, partners, and potential leads. While other companies offered CRM software as a product, Salesforce owned the CRM space as a service, creating a new paradigm in the B2B tech landscape.

LinkedIn: Microsoft's acquisition of LinkedIn solidified its presence in the professional networking space, turning LinkedIn into a powerhouse for B2B relationships, recruitment, and sales opportunities. LinkedIn distinguished itself by leveraging its network to offer a suite of solutions that includes marketing, hiring, and selling on a platform where professionals gather. This move allowed Microsoft to own the professional social networking space, making it an essential tool for business development.

Slack: Slack changed the way teams communicate internally by positioning itself as more than just a messaging application; it became a hub for team collaboration, integrating with various work applications and services. In a market full of communication tools, Slack stood out by offering a platform that centralizes workplace conversations and workflows. It's carved out a unique position as the go-to collaborative workspace tool in the B2B technology brandscape.

These companies have not merely filled existing niches; they have redefined them. They have done so by challenging the status quo and offering new value propositions.

Owning an opening in the brandscape is not just a strategy; it's a commitment to revolution, innovation, and customer-centricity. It's the creation of a brand identity that resonates deeply with your target audience and sets you apart from your competitors. CEOs and marketing leaders must lead this charge, recognizing that the brandscape is a stage on which their brand can shine.

To guarantee MROI, it's crucial that you not only understand the brandscape but also master it. Don't settle for belonging; find a unique space to own and craft a compelling narrative that resonates with your market. Embrace the revolution; these are the spaces where brands find their truest expressions and their most loyal advocates.

CHECK OUT THE 12 BATTLES™ READER HUB at marketingtoolsforyou.com for this free resource:

BRANDSCAPE TEMPLATE

Battle 5 Research Insights[13]

40% of survey respondents strongly agree that their marketing team has a firm grasp on their brand positioning and that of their primary competitors, leaving 60 percent that see opportunity for improvement.

---

[13] From the "2024 RedRover U.S. Middle-Market B2B Marketing Performance Study," available in the 12 Battles™ Reader Hub at marketingtoolsforyou.com.

24% strongly agree that their brand positioning is different from that of their competitors, indicating big growth potential for companies that research and take ownership of an opportunity in the brandscape.

Success Story

Precision Craft Industrial[14], an $18M nationwide manufacturing company based out of Houston, Texas, was growing by 5 percent or less a year but wanted to see its annual growth rate double. As we began our market research project with its team, we learned that it was unsure of any real differentiators it could lay claim to—a dangerous place to be because the CAC was quite high as a result. We embarked on a series of extensive customer interviews, customer surveys, and, ultimately, a brandscape analysis to determine where its brand could speak the loudest.

Our client and its competition all touted their expertise and customer service as their differentiators. What the research uncovered was an opportunity to talk about pain—that's right, pain! By the time Precision Craft's prospective engineering customers needed their services, they were in pain—the pain of lost sales and missed targets due to lack of manufacturing capacity. If those engineers couldn't produce enough products fast enough for their own growing customer base, they'd lose many of them, which would cause a ripple effect of lost sales talent and the resulting negative impact on their company culture and morale. So we put together and disseminated dozens of video stories told by Precision Craft's customers about the sleepless nights and stress they endured until Precision Craft came to the rescue. These customers broke down and shared the depths of the partnership—how Precision Craft was far more interested in them as

---

[14] Client details have been modified to respect confidentiality.

human beings than any sale. Not only did these authentic video stories break through, but our client also realized a 40 percent increase in year over year sales. Year over year qualified lead volume in the three years that followed increased by 45, 61, and 66 percent, respectively. Their new differentiator was pain relief.

Cautionary Tale

AutoTech Solutions[15], a $32M national industrial automation company, was dissatisfied with the impact its marketing was having on its growth. In our initial conversation, its team was confident in its unbeatable differentiator—advanced automation technology that no competitor could match.

However, it turned out that AutoTech's advanced technology was more of a goal than a current reality, as it was still resolving some significant issues. Its ambitious positioning had won contracts and allowed it to secure several major customers from its competitors, only to lose them within months when the technology failed to perform as promised. AutoTech's intentions were commendable. But had we known it was grappling with these technology quality issues, we would have advised postponing the marketing efforts. Instead, AutoTech suffered a reputational setback that will likely take years to recover from, which was distressing to witness. The lesson is to avoid laying claim to a brand position that is aspirational versus realistic or you risk customer churn.

START A REVOLUTION: OWN AN OPENING IN THE BRANDSCAPE.

---

[15] Client details have been modified to respect confidentiality.

12 BATTLES™ FRAMEWORK

1. YOU **ACCEPT** THAT YOU DESERVE AND WILL ACHIEVE GUARANTEED MARKETING OUTCOMES.

2. YOU **ACKNOWLEDGE** THAT YOU DON'T REALLY KNOW THY CUSTOMER.

3. YOU **CHAMPION** MARKET RESEARCH AS A DO-OR-DIE INVESTMENT.

4. YOU **EMBRACE** THE POWER OF ATTRIBUTION MODELING AND STOP ACCEPTING BAD DATA.

5. YOU **OWN** AN OPENING IN THE BRANDSCAPE.

6. YOU **TORCH** YOUR EXISTING STRATEGY UNAPOLOGETICALLY IF NEEDED.

7. YOU **ADVOCATE** FOR AN INVESTMENT IN EACH STAGE OF THE CUSTOMER JOURNEY.

8. YOU **CHALLENGE** YOUR TEAM TO MAKE POWERFUL STRATEGIC SHIFTS GROUNDED IN RESEARCH VERSUS TRADITION.

9. YOU **PREACH** THE GOOD WORD OF DISCIPLINED OPTIMIZATION.

10. YOU **COMMIT** TO BUILDING A PAY-FOR-PERFORMANCE TEAM AROUND YOUR STRATEGY; NOT VICE VERSA.

11. YOU **REQUIRE** A POWERFUL MARKETING DASHBOARD AND DOCUMENTED PROCESSES.

12. YOU **INSPIRE** YOUR TEAM TO STAND BEHIND THEIR MROI PROJECTIONS.

BATTLE 6 : YOU **TORCH** YOUR EXISTING STRATEGY UNAPOLOGETICALLY IF NEEDED

Battle 6

Battle 6 implores you to torch your existing strategy unapologetically if needed.

The ability to adapt and evolve is essential for survival. As a CEO or marketing leader of a middle-market B2B company, you may find yourself at a crossroads where the need for change becomes evident. Sometimes, this change isn't just about tweaking a few processes or making incremental adjustments; it's about unapologetically torching your existing marketing strategy and starting anew.

> **SOMETIMES, THE NEED FOR CHANGE ISN'T JUST ABOUT TWEAKING A FEW PROCESSES OR MAKING INCREMENTAL ADJUSTMENTS; IT'S ABOUT UNAPOLOGETICALLY TORCHING YOUR EXISTING MARKETING STRATEGY AND STARTING ANEW.**

If you're familiar with the book *Traction* and the EOS (Entrepreneurial Operating System) model developed by Gino Wickman and used by many middle-market companies across the country, then you probably know the principle of "hitting the ceiling." This is where the strategies that served you well in the past no longer work for you— likely because you've grown to a point where strategic adjustments are necessary. For example, where centralized decision making once worked, the CEO must now build and empower a professional leadership team because, thanks to growth, they are now the bottleneck. The same holds true in marketing. Perhaps you have tapped the extent of the PPC opportunity in your niche, or advancements in Google's algorithm have caused your SEO strategy to tank, or maybe the consistent email campaigns that worked three years ago are now getting lost in all the digital noise. You must adapt or die.

When you are unable to put your finger on what is not working in your marketing strategy, often it makes sense to start fresh.

Pros and Cons

The Pros of Torching Your Existing Strategy Unapologetically

Before jumping into this revolutionary approach, let's first explore the advantages of torching your existing marketing strategy unapologetically.

Innovation through fresh perspective: When you decisively discard an outdated strategy, you embrace the potential for innovation. It's an opportunity to re-evaluate your value proposition, explore new market segments, and consider technologies that could redefine your business operations. You completely reimagine your business model to tap into unexplored opportunities that drive growth.

Securing competitive advantage: A bold strategic shift positions your company as a market leader. By adopting emergent technologies or pioneering new business models, you set industry standards and shape customer expectations. This leap transforms your brand into a beacon for innovation, attracting not just customers but top-tier talent and investors who are drawn to trailblazing companies.

Proactive adaptation to market trends: Agile companies that pivot quickly in response to market trends can seize opportunities that others miss. By staying ahead of the curve, you can adapt your product offerings, go-to-market strategies, and customer experience to the evolving demands of the market, ensuring that your business remains relevant and competitive.

Enhancing employee engagement and talent attraction: A culture that encourages challenging the status quo can invigorate employees. It shows a commitment to growth and personal development, which attracts innovative thinkers and retains those who are eager to contribute to meaningful change. Engaged employees are more likely to be productive, committed, and passionate advocates for your company.

The Cons and Risks of Torching Your Existing Strategy Unapologetically

While the benefits are enticing, it's essential to acknowledge the potential cons and risks associated with torching your existing marketing strategy unapologetically.

Navigating resistance to change and employee disruption: Organizational inertia is a formidable obstacle. Altering your company's course can unsettle your team; employees and management alike may resist abandoning familiar sales and marketing processes for unknowns. This unease can manifest in various ways, from a dip in morale to a reluctance to fully engage with the new direction. In some cases, this may even lead to increased staff turnover as individuals seek environments with familiar routines.

Change management strategies must be employed to address fears, communicate the vision, and transition the team smoothly to new ways of working. It's crucial to invest in comprehensive training and support to ensure that your team not only understands the new strategy but is also fully equipped to execute it.

First, be transparent. Use open, frequent communication to explain why changes are needed and what they will involve. Allow employees to voice concerns. By doing so, the transition becomes a shared journey rather than a mandate. Next, involve team members in the change process. Gather their input and ideas, and let them be part of decision making. This inclusion not only makes the change more acceptable but also leverages their insights for better solutions. Then, provide hands-on training and support. Introduce new tools or methods in interactive sessions, and offer resources for team members to learn at their own pace. Align the new strategy with clear personal development paths to help employees see the change as an opportunity for growth rather than a disruption to be weathered. Finally, set up a feedback loop. Regularly check in with your team to see how they're adapting, and be ready to adjust your approach based on their experiences and suggestions. It's about transforming potential disruption into a positive evolution for both the team and the individual.

Preparing for strategic investments: Adopting a new marketing strategy often entails upfront investments in areas such as technology upgrades, rebranding, overhauling your website and other digital assets, internal skills development, and/or upgrading your marketing agency relationship. While there is an inherent financial outlay, a meticulously researched strategy allows you to anticipate these costs and understand their role in driving predictable returns. With a clear

MROI timeline based on your market research, you can proceed with confidence, knowing that these calculated investments are steps toward future profitability.

Managing team expectations amidst well-informed changes: Embarking on a new strategy, even with extensive market research and a well-crafted plan, still carries elements of the unknown. While your research will provide a solid foundation, the market can be unpredictable and customer behavior can shift. It's important to be prepared for adjustments even when your strategy is data-driven. This means setting realistic expectations, communicating to your team that pivots may be necessary, and monitoring outcomes closely to ensure your approach remains aligned with actual market responses. Stay ready to refine your tactics with precision based on the robust data you've gathered and the insights you continue to acquire.

To Tweak or to Torch?

When to Optimize Your Existing Strategy

Optimizing your strategy involves making incremental improvements and adjustments to your existing plan to enhance its effectiveness. Consider optimization when you have experienced or are experiencing:

- **Historical success with your current strategy:** If analytics show that certain campaigns or tactics that have been highly successful in the past are now experiencing a gradual decline in conversion rates or customer engagement, it may be time to refresh those areas while retaining the core of what works in your marketing strategy.

- **Shifts in customer behavior:** If market intelligence reveals that your B2B customers are changing the way they engage with your services, such as a noticeable preference for interactive content over white papers or increased activity on professional networks like LinkedIn rather than traditional industry events, your strategy may simply need to adapt to these new interactive platforms.

- **Budgetary restraints:** If financial reports suggest limited budgets and you cannot afford a comprehensive strategy overhaul, look for cost-effective optimizations, such as automating specific marketing tasks to increase efficiency. Consider cutting any tactic that isn't producing or substantially contributing to a positive MROI, but always bear in mind the impact the cuts will have on the customer journey.

- **Incremental innovation needs:** Industry reporting or your own competitive shopping might show that competitors are adopting new technologies or trends. If your strategies are falling behind, testing new innovations could be necessary to stay competitive. The key is to ensure that only a maximum of 20 percent of your marketing investment is allocated to testing new innovative strategies while 80 percent remains in proven strategies.

- **Team dynamics and morale at risk:** Employee feedback and performance reviews might reveal that the marketing and/or sales team is highly committed to the current strategy and showing positive morale, indicating that a strategy optimization could be more effective and less disruptive than a complete overhaul. Just be sure not to let fear of change derail a dire need for a strategy pivot.

- **Short-term market fluctuations:** Economic reports or sudden shifts in market dynamics, like new regulations or temporary supply chain disruptions, may necessitate quick adaptations in strategy rather than a full-scale revision, preserving the core while adjusting to any new conditions—especially if the shifts are temporary.

Leverage these best practices to determine when your marketing strategy needs optimization versus mass destruction, and implement targeted adjustments to enhance effectiveness.

When to Torch Your Existing Strategy

In certain scenarios, incremental improvements are not enough; instead you must radically reimagine your strategy. It's time to consider a comprehensive overhaul when any of these red flags appear:

- **Market misalignment:** Market research shows that key decision makers in your target businesses no longer find that your content resonates or engagement rates with your thought leadership materials have plummeted. This suggests that your brand's messaging is out of sync with your audience's current challenges and goals.

- **Persistent performance decline:** Data analytics reveal a consistent downward trend in lead generation and conversion rates, especially if coupled with feedback indicating that your marketing messages fail to differentiate your offerings in a saturated market.

- **Outpaced by technological innovation:** Emerging technologies such as AI-enhanced analytics or blockchain-based customer verification are redefining engagement in your industry, and your marketing methods haven't adapted to utilize these tools for targeted outreach, personalization, and security. Or a new market entrant is reshaping expectations with a radical approach, like using machine learning to predict customer needs, rendering your traditional marketing approaches less effective.

- **Competitive threats:** Competitive analysis reveals that your rivals are capturing market share by leveraging more sophisticated digital marketing techniques or utilizing data analytics in ways that significantly outperform your current marketing efforts.

- **Seismic industry shifts:** There are sweeping changes in industry standards or customer procurement processes have shifted (like a move toward subscription models over traditional purchasing), and your marketing has not adapted to address these new paradigms.

- **Leadership changes:** A new C-suite executive or marketing head arrives with a mandate for change, especially if they bring insights from markets or demographics that your organization has not previously tapped into, signaling that a different marketing approach is needed to align with new business objectives.

Reacting to these signs with a complete strategy revision—backed by deep market research—can rejuvenate your brand's positioning, offering a chance to re-establish your business as a leading voice in your industry.

> **REACTING TO THESE SIGNS WITH A COMPLETE STRATEGY REVISION CAN REJUVENATE YOUR BRAND'S POSITIONING, OFFERING A CHANCE TO RE-ESTABLISH YOUR BUSINESS AS A LEADING VOICE IN YOUR INDUSTRY.**

Assessing the Need for External Expertise

There are times when the scale and complexity of transformational change exceed in-house expertise. Here's when seeking external professionals is sensible:

- **Filling expertise gaps:** Should your change initiative demand specialized skills that your team lacks, external specialists can provide the necessary expertise.

- **Accelerating implementation:** When timely execution is essential to meet strategic objectives, leveraging outside resources can quicken the pace.

- **Objective problem-solving:** A fresh set of eyes can offer new perspectives, objectivity, and innovative solutions to persistent issues that have eluded resolution.

- **Mitigating risks:** Drawing on the experiences of those who've successfully navigated similar transitions can help minimize missteps and create efficiency.

- **Specialized skill sets for advanced tactics:** When new marketing strategies involve sophisticated techniques or platforms that your team isn't well-versed in, such as predictive analytics, advanced PPC optimization, leveraging the Google Analytics platform, or advanced technical (versus on-page) SEO tactics, external experts can fill these skill gaps, ensuring your strategy is executed with the highest level of expertise while reducing marketing investment waste.

- **Objective strategy assessment:** An external viewpoint can be critical in assessing the effectiveness of your current strategy. Professionals outside your organization can conduct impartial audits and bring insights that might be overlooked internally due to inherent biases.

- **Navigating complex integrations:** If your marketing strategy requires integrating complex new systems or software that interact with multiple business functions, external experts can manage these integrations smoothly, ensuring systems work seamlessly together without disrupting existing operations.

- **Accountability:** Many leaders find it simpler to hold an external team accountable for guaranteed outcomes.

When bringing in external marketing experts, find the right fit for your team. A good marketing agency can fill in where your team is lacking, bring in new ideas, and help you get things done more quickly and effectively. They've been through this kind of change before and can guide you through it, reducing the chances of costly mistakes. So take a close look at what your organization aims to achieve and consider how an external team could support your goals. If you do decide to partner with an agency, check out the 12 Battles™ Reader Hub for 20 questions to ask potential agency partners to ensure you're getting your money's worth.

CHECK OUT THE 12 BATTLES™ READER HUB at marketingtoolsforyou.com for this free resource:

20 QUESTIONS TO ASK AGENCY CONTENDERS

Battle 6 Research Insights[16]

54% of survey respondents say they are willing to completely walk away from their current marketing strategy and start over to improve their MROI. This might inspire you to do the same if required. Forty-six percent are either unwilling or on the fence.

58% of those who are unwilling or on the fence cite "some of it is working" as the top reason to stick with what

---

[16] From the "2024 RedRover U.S. Middle-Market B2B Marketing Performance Study," available in the 12 Battles™ Reader Hub at marketingtoolsforyou.com.

they have. The next most popular reasons are "I've invested too much in it already" and "if better executed, I feel that it would succeed" at 33 percent each. Be sure not to let confirmation bias—the tendency to interpret new evidence as confirmation of existing beliefs—slow you down from torching what's not working.

Success Story

Spotlight Connections[17], a $2M firm specializing in connecting keynote speakers and brand ambassadors within a range of sectors, acknowledged the risk of its heavy reliance on in-person events at a time when virtual events were beginning to pick up steam. To expand its reach, it embarked on an ambitious marketing strategy targeting higher technological industries, such as virtual event platforms, online education providers, and digital health services.

The strategic shift was visionary. As COVID-19 brought the traditional in-person event industry to a standstill, the versatility in Spotlight Connections' marketing approach became a lifeline. Nearly every one of its in-person contracts dried up, and it struggled to make payroll. Leveraging the insights from its comprehensive pre-pandemic market research, it redirected efforts toward sectors that were experiencing a surge in demand due to the new remote work reality.

This pivot led to a threefold increase in MQLs in just three months along with a 77 percent decrease in lead acquisition costs. Our charge was to hand over a solid, adaptable marketing campaign to its in-house team—one that was in line with its cost-saving priorities. Spotlight Connections was left with an efficient strategy, an active pipeline in resilient industries, and, most importantly, a diversified approach to safeguard against future industry disruptions.

---

[17] Client details have been modified to respect confidentiality.

And while it certainly had to torch its existing strategy when the pandemic hit, its choice since then to stick with the dramatically overhauled strategy took real courage. While it was no doubt tempting to accept all that old business back post-pandemic, to ensure it doesn't have a repeat situation, it now only allows a certain percentage of bookings to come from in-person events. The digital event lead-generation strategy is now the biggest part of Spotlight Connections' marketing plan.

Cautionary Tale

A national membership organization, venerable at 50 years old with an average member age of 65-plus, recognized the need to rejuvenate its appeal to attract younger members—the next generation of members. Collaborating closely with its team, we undertook extensive research to pave a thoughtful path forward. We aimed to reframe the brand to resonate with Generation X and Millennials, understanding that not only would this torch its existing marketing strategy, it also would transform its service offerings into a far higher technological delivery system to meet the expectations of these emerging member groups.

The CEO was an advocate for this evolution, envisioning a vibrant future for the organization. However, the proposal faced resistance from the board and leadership team, who found the breadth of change daunting. Despite the CEO's enthusiasm based on our research and our shared vision for renewal, the resistance reflected a deep-seated hesitation to depart from long-established norms.

In the end, the organization chose not to proceed. While we didn't agree, we certainly understood. This outcome was risky but not uncommon in institutions with deep-rooted histories. We appreciated the complexities involved in aligning diverse stakeholder groups with a bold new direction and respected their decision to maintain their course, hoping there was still time to right the ship when the issue no doubt resurfaced.

> **START A REVOLUTION: TORCH YOUR EXISTING STRATEGY UNAPOLOGETICALLY IF NEEDED.**

12 BATTLES™ FRAMEWORK

1 YOU **ACCEPT** THAT YOU DESERVE AND WILL ACHIEVE GUARANTEED MARKETING OUTCOMES.

2 YOU **ACKNOWLEDGE** THAT YOU DON'T REALLY KNOW THY CUSTOMER.

3 YOU **CHAMPION** MARKET RESEARCH AS A DO-OR-DIE INVESTMENT.

4 YOU **EMBRACE** THE POWER OF ATTRIBUTION MODELING AND STOP ACCEPTING BAD DATA.

5 YOU **OWN** AN OPENING IN THE BRANDSCAPE.

6 YOU **TORCH** YOUR EXISTING STRATEGY UNAPOLOGETICALLY IF NEEDED.

7 YOU **ADVOCATE** FOR AN INVESTMENT IN EACH STAGE OF THE CUSTOMER JOURNEY.

8 YOU **CHALLENGE** YOUR TEAM TO MAKE POWERFUL STRATEGIC SHIFTS GROUNDED IN RESEARCH VERSUS TRADITION.

9 YOU **PREACH** THE GOOD WORD OF DISCIPLINED OPTIMIZATION.

10 YOU **COMMIT** TO BUILDING A PAY-FOR-PERFORMANCE TEAM AROUND YOUR STRATEGY; NOT VICE VERSA.

11 YOU **REQUIRE** A POWERFUL MARKETING DASHBOARD AND DOCUMENTED PROCESSES.

12 YOU **INSPIRE** YOUR TEAM TO STAND BEHIND THEIR MROI PROJECTIONS.

BATTLE 7 : YOU **ADVOCATE** FOR AN INVESTMENT IN EACH STAGE OF THE CUSTOMER JOURNEY

Battle 7

Battle 7 involves you advocating for an investment in each stage of the customer journey.

The customer journey is a comprehensive framework that mirrors the buyer's path, illustrating the stages a prospect goes through before becoming a loyal customer. It typically comprises four key stages:

1. **Awareness:** At the initial stage of the journey, businesses strive to create brand awareness and capture the attention of potential customers. Strategies include content marketing, social media engagement, and SEO.

2. **Consideration:** In this stage, prospects are actively exploring solutions to their problems. Companies must provide valuable content, engage in thought leadership, and demonstrate their expertise to be considered a viable option.

3. **Conversion:** The middle of the journey is where leads transition into customers. Convincing prospects to make a purchase is the primary goal, and it involves effective nurturing and compelling offers.

4. **Post-purchase:** Once converted, customers enter the post-purchase stage. Here, the focus shifts to delivering exceptional customer experiences, maintaining relationships, and encouraging repeat business and referrals.

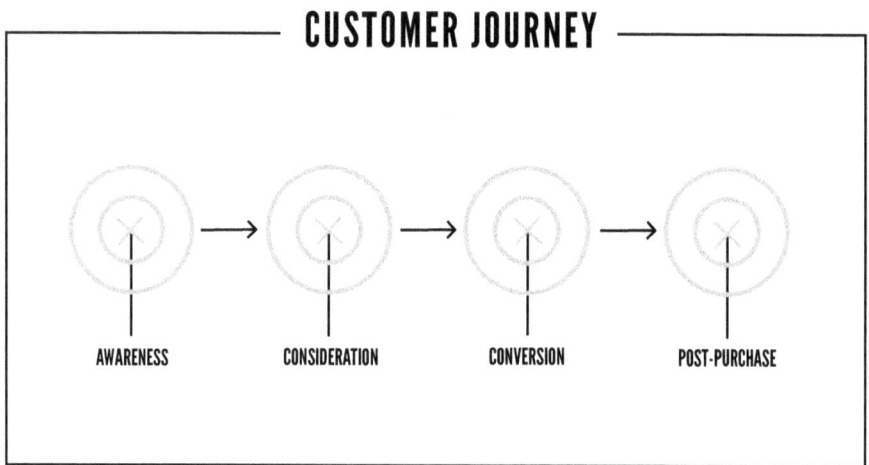

CUSTOMER JOURNEY

AWARENESS   CONSIDERATION   CONVERSION   POST-PURCHASE

The Criticality of Investing at Each Stage of the Customer Journey

All too often, companies make the mistake of investing only in the consideration stage when prospects have a high intent to make a purchase. I get it. That's low-hanging fruit. But this strategy misses all the opportunities further up the funnel and limits your ability to scale. It's short-sighted.

> INVESTING ONLY IN PROSPECTS WITH A HIGH
> INTENT TO PURCHASE MISSES ALL THE
> OPPORTUNITIES FURTHER UP THE FUNNEL
> AND LIMITS YOUR ABILITY TO SCALE.

As a B2B marketing leader or CEO, you must battle this thinking. Each stage of the customer journey requires an investment to build a marketing engine that truly scales your company to its fullest potential.

The customer journey represents the lifeline of a company's relationship with its clientele. Neglecting any of these crucial stages leaves opportunities for growth, customer satisfaction, and business sustainability untapped.

Why Invest at the Awareness Stage?

Building a strong foundation: Investing in the awareness stage sets the foundation for long-term success. Building brand awareness ensures that your company is on the radar of potential customers, making it more likely that they will consider your offerings when the need arises. An effective awareness strategy establishes your brand as an industry authority, instilling trust and credibility.

Capturing a wider audience: The awareness stage allows you to reach a broad audience, including those who might not have an immediate need for your products or services. By casting a wider net, you create opportunities to nurture prospects over time, ensuring that your brand remains top of mind when they're ready to make a purchasing decision.

Generating demand: Investment in awareness often involves content marketing, which educates your audience about industry trends, challenges, and potential solutions. As a result, you create demand for your products or services, even among those who weren't initially aware of their need for them.

Feeding the journey: The awareness stage serves as the journey's entry point. It's the source of leads that will move through the subsequent stages. Without a continuous investment in generating awareness, the journey can stagnate, impeding growth and revenue generation.

Why Invest at the Consideration Stage?

Guiding the decision-making process: The consideration stage is where prospects actively research and compare solutions. Investing in this stage allows you to influence their decision-making process. Providing high-quality, informative content positions your company as a trusted advisor and helps prospects navigate their options. Email, influencer, and customer review strategies are common in this stage.

Qualifying leads: By nurturing prospects in the consideration stage, you qualify leads effectively. Not all leads are equal, and dedicating resources to this stage enables you to identify which prospects are most likely to convert. This, in turn, optimizes your sales efforts and enhances efficiency.

Creating a competitive advantage: Competitors are vying for the attention of the same prospects. Investing in consideration-stage marketing gives you a competitive advantage by showcasing your unique value propositions and differentiating your offerings.

Building relationships: The consideration stage is an opportunity to build relationships with potential customers. Engaging with them, addressing their pain points, and providing valuable insights fosters trust and goodwill that extends into the conversion and retention stages.

Why Invest at the Conversion Stage?

Turning leads into revenue: The goal of any marketing effort is to generate revenue. The conversion stage is where leads become paying customers. Investing in this stage ensures that your marketing efforts translate into tangible business outcomes.

Shortening sales cycles: Investment at the conversion stage streamlines the sales process. By providing prospects with compelling offers, clear calls to action, personalized experiences, product or service guarantees, a simplified check-out process, and responsive support, you reduce the time it takes for them to decide. Abandoned cart recovery and retargeting strategies are also common in this stage.

Demonstrating MROI: Measuring MROI becomes more straightforward when resources are dedicated to the conversion stage. Marketing leaders and CEOs can clearly track the impact of their marketing investments in terms of customer acquisition, revenue, and profitability.

Maintaining continuity: The conversion stage marks the transition from prospect to customer. Investing here is crucial for maintaining continuity in engagement and ensuring that the customer's experience is seamless and positive from initial contact through to the purchase.

Why Invest at the Post-Purchase Stage?

Maximizing customer LTV: Retaining existing customers is usually far more cost-effective than acquiring new ones. Investing in the post-purchase stage focuses on delivering exceptional customer experiences, which leads to repeat business, upselling, and cross-selling opportunities.

Building brand advocacy: Satisfied customers become advocates for your brand, recommending your products or services to others. Investment in the post-purchase stage turns customers into loyal brand advocates, contributing to organic growth.

Reducing churn: Customer retention efforts aim to reduce churn rates, which are a significant drain on resources. Retaining customers through ongoing engagement, support, and value-added services lowers churn and stabilizes revenue streams.

Driving improvements: Investment in the post-purchase stage often involves data analysis and feedback collection. This information is invaluable for identifying areas for improvement, enhancing product offerings, and refining marketing strategies based on real customer insights.

In essence, a marketing leader's or CEO's commitment to investing at every stage of the customer journey is a strategic choice that drives growth, fosters customer satisfaction, and, ultimately, secures the future prosperity of the business.

It All Matters

Now, you may be asking how this factors into the creation of a results-guaranteed marketing plan? Can you track your performance at each stage?

At its core, marketing is both an art and a science. While data-driven decisions form the bedrock of any strategy, there's an art to understanding the nuances of human behavior, to building brand stories, and to crafting messages that resonate with your customers. Some elements of your marketing plan, such as brand awareness ads, may not offer easily measurable MROI, yet they're indispensable.

Why? Because every touchpoint, every interaction, and every message contributes to the larger narrative of the brand. It's like constructing a puzzle; while some pieces might not seem significant in isolation, they're crucial to completing the overall picture. An over-reliance on only the measurable can lead to tunnel vision. The key is to ensure that the gains from the strategies where clear returns can be measured more than cover the investment in the unmeasurable.

Investing at each stage of the customer journey is not just an expenditure; it's an investment in the growth, resilience, and long-term success of your business. Marketing leaders and CEOs who recognize the value of a holistic approach that encompasses awareness, consideration, conversion, and post-purchase are better positioned to navigate the dynamic business landscape.

In today's marketplace, where customer relationships and brand reputation are paramount, investing at each stage of the customer journey is not just a best practice—it's a strategic imperative.

Battle 7 Research Insights[18]

42% of all survey respondents strongly agree that they invest sufficiently in each stage of the customer journey—from awareness to consideration to conversion to post-purchase. Another 42 percent agree while 15 percent are neutral, unsure, or disagree. As a company's headcount increases, and, therefore, its size, so does respondent confidence in proper customer journey investment. In fact, for companies between 501 and 1000 employees, 66 percent of respondents strongly agree that they do this well.

76% of survey respondents who invest 6.1 to 7 percent of revenue in marketing, in particular, strongly agree that they invest sufficiently in each stage of the customer journey. It's no coincidence that MROI also improves as marketing investment increases. The takeaway for smaller companies is that a strong, early investment in all four stages of the customer journey often expedites growth.

---

[18] From the "2024 RedRover U.S. Middle-Market B2B Marketing Performance Study," available in the 12 Battles™ Reader Hub at marketingtoolsforyou.com.

very short

Success Story

Innovative Industrial Analytics[19], a $35M data analysis and consulting firm headquartered in the Midwest, had long prioritized brand visibility in the competitive technology consulting market. However, while CEO Lisa had championed the necessity of brand awareness, she acknowledged the company's shortfall in addressing the subsequent stages of the customer journey. Recognizing the need for a more balanced investment strategy, Lisa reached out to RedRover for a comprehensive approach to engaging potential customers throughout the customer journey, from initial awareness to post-purchase advocacy, aiming for a more tangible and measurable MROI.

Lisa was open to the idea that the investment should be better distributed. The final breakdown looked like this:

- Awareness: 40 percent
- Consideration: 45 percent
- Conversion: 5 percent
- Post-purchase engagement: 10 percent

In the first five months after the campaign launch, 226 leads were generated from the investment in the consideration stage of the customer journey, compared to just 21 from the awareness stage, although that number was up as well. That was 226 MQLs from companies who were actively considering a purchase at an average customer LTV of $50,000 each. It's important to understand that while investing in the consideration stage typically yields more immediate results, investment in the awareness stage is crucial as it lays the foundation for enhanced results in the consideration and conversion stages.

---

[19] Client details have been modified to respect confidentiality.

Tip: A typical B2B marketing budget allocates more resources to the awareness and consideration stages where content creation, brand positioning, and lead generation are critical. Conversion and post-purchase stages might see investments in CRM systems, customer service platforms, and retention campaigns if these are not already in place.

Cautionary Tale

LogiSphere Dynamics[20], an innovative $8M start-up in the logistics space, recognized the potential of improving its customer acquisition process to significantly impact its bottom line. With an average yearly transaction size of $65,000, the acquisition of just a few additional MQLs per week could lead to substantial growth within the company.

The initial objective was clear: Generate five new MQLs per week. The president, Richard, was confident in a divided strategy where marketing would solely drive lead generation and the sales team would independently convert these leads into sales. This approach, however, underestimated the critical importance of investing in every touchpoint of the customer journey.

When leads failed to convert as expected, an in-depth analysis was undertaken. The insights were revealing. Sales representatives took an average of five business days to initiate contact; the company's unique value was not being effectively communicated; and follow-up was inconsistent, with more than a quarter of the leads left in limbo. In addition, the company was seeing a churn of new customers because of friction in the customer onboarding process.

Acknowledging these challenges, Richard agreed to a comprehensive sales and marketing alignment inventory, which underscored the need for a cohesive strategy. We included the accounts team in this

---

[20] Client details have been modified to respect confidentiality.

inventory as well, as they were responsible for onboarding new customers. This strategic pivot emphasized the importance of a seamless transition from marketing to sales to accounts, ensuring that each lead was nurtured with the same level of care and precision as it was generated.

Investment across all stages of the customer journey became the new mantra for LogiSphere Dynamics. By aligning sales and marketing efforts, the company not only improved lead conversion rates but also fostered a culture of collaboration that propelled it to new heights in the logistics industry.

START A REVOLUTION: ADVOCATE FOR AN INVESTMENT IN EACH STAGE OF THE CUSTOMER JOURNEY.

12 BATTLES™ FRAMEWORK

1 YOU **ACCEPT** THAT YOU DESERVE AND WILL ACHIEVE GUARANTEED MARKETING OUTCOMES.

2 YOU **ACKNOWLEDGE** THAT YOU DON'T REALLY KNOW THY CUSTOMER.

3 YOU **CHAMPION** MARKET RESEARCH AS A DO-OR-DIE INVESTMENT.

4 YOU **EMBRACE** THE POWER OF ATTRIBUTION MODELING AND STOP ACCEPTING BAD DATA.

5 YOU **OWN** AN OPENING IN THE BRANDSCAPE.

6 YOU **TORCH** YOUR EXISTING STRATEGY UNAPOLOGETICALLY IF NEEDED.

7 YOU **ADVOCATE** FOR AN INVESTMENT IN EACH STAGE OF THE CUSTOMER JOURNEY.

8 YOU **CHALLENGE** YOUR TEAM TO MAKE POWERFUL STRATEGIC SHIFTS GROUNDED IN RESEARCH VERSUS TRADITION.

9 YOU **PREACH** THE GOOD WORD OF DISCIPLINED OPTIMIZATION.

10 YOU **COMMIT** TO BUILDING A PAY-FOR-PERFORMANCE TEAM AROUND YOUR STRATEGY; NOT VICE VERSA.

11 YOU **REQUIRE** A POWERFUL MARKETING DASHBOARD AND DOCUMENTED PROCESSES.

12 YOU **INSPIRE** YOUR TEAM TO STAND BEHIND THEIR MROI PROJECTIONS.

BATTLE 8 : YOU **CHALLENGE** YOUR TEAM TO MAKE POWERFUL STRATEGIC SHIFTS GROUNDED IN RESEARCH VERSUS TRADITION

Battle 8

Battle 8 necessitates you challenging your team to make powerful strategic shifts grounded in research rather than tradition.

The War Room Strategy Debate

With your market research completed, your attribution model selected, your place in the brandscape solidified, and your commitment made to full customer journey investment, you are ready to craft your new results-guaranteed marketing strategy. For this, you'll need to select a group of marketing experts to bring into a war room for two half days for the purpose of arriving at your high-level go-forward strategy. We at RedRover call this session a "war room strategy debate." Your team will engage in a focused, no-holds-barred session designed to dissect, challenge, and fortify marketing plans, ensuring that every aspect of the strategy is battle-tested and ready to conquer the market.

> **THE WAR ROOM STRATEGY DEBATE IS WHERE YOUR TEAM IS ENGAGED IN A NO-HOLDS-BARRED DEBATE DESIGNED TO DISSECT, CHALLENGE, AND FORTIFY YOUR MARKETING PLANS, ENSURING THAT EVERY ASPECT OF THE STRATEGY IS BATTLE-TESTED AND READY TO CONQUER THE MARKET.**

The experts invited to the war room strategy debate, from inside or outside your organization or a combination of the two, need to represent each of the 10 areas of marketing specialty that could fall into your B2B marketing plan, including:

1. SEO specialist
2. SEM (search engine marketing)/PPC specialist
3. Public relations specialist
4. Branding specialist
5. Content specialist
6. Design/creative specialist
7. Email marketing specialist
8. Social media specialist
9. Website conversion specialist
10. Event marketing/trade show specialist

The odds are that you don't have each of these 10 specialties in-house, which means you'll need external support. It is imperative that you have specialists, not generalists, in the room for each marketing specialty you might conceivably include in your results-guaranteed marketing plan; otherwise, you are in danger of biasing the final plan by stacking the deck with advocates for the strategies you or your team prefer or have traditionally included in your marketing plan versus the strategies that will be most effective.

> IT IS IMPERATIVE THAT YOU HAVE SPECIALISTS IN THE ROOM FOR EACH MARKETING SPECIALTY YOU MIGHT CONCEIVABLY INCLUDE IN YOUR PLAN; OTHERWISE, YOU ARE IN DANGER OF BIASING THE FINAL PLAN BY STACKING THE DECK WITH ADVOCATES FOR THE STRATEGIES YOU OR YOUR TEAM PREFER VERSUS THE STRATEGIES THAT WILL BE MOST EFFECTIVE.

In preparation for your war room strategy debate, assign pre-work to the participants, including reviewing the Customer Journey Pre-Read found in the 12 Battles™ Reader Hub in order to ground them in an understanding of the customer journey. In this pre-work, they'll receive a copy of all of the research and data insights—both the data and your synthesis of the key findings. To recap, here's the research they should receive in advance:

1. Internal and external stakeholder interviews
2. Competitive surveillance including reputation scan and indexing
3. Value proposition comparison
4. Offer strategy evaluation
5. Sales and marketing alignment inventory
6. Marketing performance audit
7. Customer transaction analysis
8. Current, lost, and prospective customer survey

CHECK OUT THE 12 BATTLES™ READER HUB at marketingtoolsforyou.com for this free resource:

WAR ROOM STRATEGY DEBATE CUSTOMER JOURNEY PRE-READ

All participants must review this information in preparation for the session and come to the debate armed with the top three marketing strategies that they believe the data supports and will generate the strongest measurable MROI in year one. With 10 specialists, you ought to have a total of 30 strategy recommendations. Participants also should come with their analysis of the MROI that they believe each of these strategies will generate in year one including the math to show how they arrived at that projection. Participants should document their pre-work on three flip charts that they bring to the debate—one flip chart per strategy. They will present their findings formally in the debate—a maximum of 15 minutes per person or 5 minutes per strategy. *Important*: If they don't prepare, they should not attend. Ill-prepared participants could sway the conversation in a way that isn't supported by your research.

CHECK OUT THE 12 BATTLES™ READER HUB at marketingtoolsforyou.com for this free resource:

WAR ROOM STRATEGY DEBATE EMAIL TEMPLATE

Bring your war room strategy debate team together for two half days. Record this meeting using a platform that will also transcribe it so that you don't need to take notes. Have fun with the day. The agenda that follows has a *Hunger Games* theme. Just as a battle royale determined the victor in the *Hunger Games* movies, so must your team battle-test your strategies to determine the winners and losers. As such, attendees are called "tributes"; your meeting room is the "arena"; and the strategy prioritization exercise is the "reaping." Consider using this or your own favorite theme and bring in some decor or props to add amusement to the day.

War Room Strategy Debate Agenda: "May the odds be ever in your favor"[21]

Following is your agenda for each day, with facilitation notes for each section.

Day 1 8:00–10:30: **Tribute (attendee) presentations and MROI pitches**

- Kick off the day by asking each "tribute" to place their flip charts on the walls of the arena (your meeting room) so that they can be seen by all other tributes. On the top right of the flip charts, number each from 1 to 30. Then give each of your 10 tributes 15 minutes to pitch their recommendations and MROI projections, proving their worth in the games.

Day 1 10:30–10:40: **Replenishing supplies (break)**

Day 1 10:40–11:00: **The reaping (prioritization exercise)**

- Tributes spend 15 to 20 quiet minutes walking around the arena and examining all the flip charts, ultimately marking their allegiance by placing their initials in the top left-hand corner of the flip charts representing the top three strategies they believe will ensure victory (drive measurable MROI).

- If they believe that any of the strategies should be combined because they are both simply nuances of the same idea and complement one another, they should note that on the flip chart as well (e.g., combine #3 with #7).

Day 1 11:00–12:30: **The alliance formation (top strategy debate)**

- Evaluate whether potential alliances (strategy combinations)

---

[21] Collins, Suzanne. *The Hunger Games.* Scholastic Press, 2008.

make sense. If they do, move those two flip charts together and total the votes for both strategies.

- Identify up to 15 strategies with the most votes and move them to the cornucopia (the center of the room) where they can be easily seen by all tributes. Then, facilitate a debate where your team argues the merits and risks of each of the top performing strategies for roughly 5 minutes per strategy. Make sure you hear from everyone in the room, especially those from the districts further out (the quieter voices). Note that the first time you facilitate a war room strategy debate, this step in the process may take longer than the 90 minutes allotted in the agenda. In time, you'll get faster at your facilitation of this section.

- Ask for another vote, this time with the intention of narrowing the field to a max of 10 strategies, though your number may be smaller. Again votes are cast by tributes placing their initials on the flip charts of the top three strategies they believe to be strongest—this time in the lower left-hand corner.

Day 2 8:00–11:45 (with a 10-minute break in the middle): **The quarter quell (top 10 questions)**

Ask the tributes the following 10 questions about each of your top 10 (or fewer depending on where you landed on Day 1) strategies. These questions are designed to provoke thoughtful analysis and ensure that the strategies discussed are robust, viable, and align with the Capital's (company's) objectives. They will help your tributes critically evaluate each strategy from multiple angles and consider both the potential rewards and the inherent risks. You will likely cut some of the strategies as you go, as only the strongest should survive:

1. **Grounded in research:** Is this strategy grounded in the research? How so?

2. **Feasibility analysis:** What are the potential obstacles in implementing this strategy, and how can we overcome them?

3. **Alignment check:** How does this strategy align with our overall business objectives and brand values? How does it align with the sales team's strategies and goals? Will this strategy positively impact the outcomes of any of our other top strategies under consideration?

4. **Market impact:** What is the expected impact of this strategy on our market position and competitive edge?

5. **Customer value:** How will this strategy improve the customer experience?

6. **Innovation index:** Does this strategy introduce innovative practices to our marketing efforts?

7. **Customer journey:** Where in the customer journey would this strategy be most useful? (Note that stage(s) on each flip chart.)

8. **MROI detailing:** Do you agree with the MROI projections for this strategy? Where might they be flawed?

9. **Risk assessment:** What are the risks involved with this strategy, and how do we plan to mitigate them?

10. **Scalability exam:** Is this strategy scalable, and how does it fit into our long-term growth plans?

After you have answered all 10 questions for a strategy, decide as a group if you should keep or kill it. As facilitator, you get a vote, and you are also the tie-breaker when needed.

CHECK OUT THE 12 BATTLES™ READER HUB at marketingtoolsforyou.com for this free resource:

WAR ROOM STRATEGY DEBATE TOP 10 QUESTIONS

Day 2 11:45–12:25: **Identifying the mockingjays (gaps in the customer journey)**

- Armed with an agreement from the tributes on where each of the vetted strategies sits in the typical customer journey (from question #7), ask them to fill in any gaps with mockingjay-type strategies that could inspire and bring about change. What strategies should be considered or reconsidered, as they may have already been vetted and ruled out because the MROI isn't easily measurable, to ensure that you're investing sufficiently at each stage of the customer journey?

Day 2 12:25–12:45: **Building the arsenal (the foundation)**

- For each strategy still standing, quickly brainstorm the essential resources and preparations needed for its successful deployment. This is the time to ensure your arsenal is well-equipped and your defenses are strong. What foundation-building elements must be in place in order for that strategy to be successful? For example, a successful PPC campaign requires a strong high-converting website or landing page. Or, you may conclude that your social media ad campaign will not break through without first rebranding.

- Note that these investments likely won't give you a directly measurable MROI. The key to a results-guaranteed plan is to ensure that the MROI on your activities that are measurable more than pay for your activities that aren't—delivering a strong measurable MROI on your overall plan.

> ## THE KEY TO A RESULTS-GUARANTEED PLAN IS TO ENSURE THAT THE MROI ON YOUR ACTIVITIES THAT ARE MEASURABLE MORE THAN PAY FOR YOUR ACTIVITIES THAT AREN'T—DELIVERING A STRONG MEASURABLE MROI ON YOUR OVERALL PLAN.

Day 2 12:45–1:00: **The victor's tour (wrap up)**

- Thank your tributes for their bravery and contributions. Explain that your next step is to take the ideas discussed and further vet them before arriving at a final results-guaranteed marketing strategy that is battle-tested and ready for the Capitol's (company's) approval. Make it clear that not everything discussed in the arena will make the final cut, and, through this vetting process, new ideas may emerge.

- Answer any questions they have about the process going forward.

CHECK OUT THE 12 BATTLES™ READER HUB at marketingtoolsforyou.com for this free resource:

WAR ROOM STRATEGY DEBATE FACILITATION GUIDE

CHECK OUT THE 12 BATTLES™ READER HUB at marketingtoolsforyou.com for this free resource:

WAR ROOM STRATEGY DEBATE PRINTABLE TEAM AGENDA

Within two business days of completion of your war room strategy debate, while the conversation is still fresh on your mind, book an eight-hour block of focus time in a place where you won't be distracted. Your job as the marketing leader or CEO (if you're also wearing the marketing leader hat) is to take every strategy that makes the final cut and make sure it's bulletproof by answering questions like the following:

- What assumptions need to be further vetted?

- What will be necessary to ensure each strategy is successful?

- What obstacles will you encounter in executing that strategy that you can plan for in advance?

- Is the MROI analysis for that strategy sound?

- Are the sales projections for that strategy realistic, especially early on when you're still optimizing it for peak performance?

- What are the primary variables that you'll split test as part of your strategy optimization process?

- What are at least three contingency plans for each strategy if it doesn't immediately achieve the projected outcomes?

As you work to vet the strategies favored by your team, consider the importance of continual investment in new innovative strategies either to existing or new markets to ensure your marketing plan is always evolving. You may very well need to add strategies to the list for vetting that keep you innovating. The strategies of today won't set you apart tomorrow. You must always be on the hunt for the next channel, the next offer, the next messaging strategy that breaks through against current and new target markets. Think about it this way: If 80 percent of your marketing investment is in strategies that have been tested—that are proven—you have 20 percent to invest in new innovative strategies. If you commit to this breakdown of funding, you will create a culture of innovation inside your marketing team.

Then determine what strategies will indeed make the final cut. Using an organization scheme, like the following grid, allows you to see all of the gathered information in one place for ease of comparison and vetting.

SAMPLE WAR ROOM STRATEGY VETTING WORKSHEET

NAME OF STRATEGY					

DETAILED STRATEGY DESCRIPTION

FOUNDATIONAL ELEMENTS NECESSARY FOR SUCCESSFUL STRATEGY EXECUTION

Item #1	
Item #2	
Item #3	
Item #4	
Item #5	

PROJECTED OUTCOMES OVER THE YEAR

	Q1	Q2	Q3	Q4	TOTAL
MQLs	#	#	#	#	#
SQLs	#	#	#	#	#
INCREMENTAL REVENUE	$	$	$	$	$

TOTAL PROJECTED MROI

Projected Strategy Cost (Including Internal/External Labor)	$
Projected Foundational Building Elements Cost	$
Total Costs	$
Total Projected Incremental Annual Revenue	$
Projected MROI	$_____ to $1

SAMPLE WAR ROOM STRATEGY VETTING WORKSHEET

VETTING QUESTIONS
What assumptions need to be further vetted?
What will be necessary to ensure this strategy is successful?
What obstacles will we likely encounter in executing this strategy that we can plan for in advance? What are those detailed contingency plans?
Is the MROI analysis for this strategy sound?
Are the sales projections for this strategy realistic, especially early on when we're still optimizing this strategy for peak performance?
What are the primary variables that we'll split test as part of our strategy optimization process?
What are at least three contingency plans for this strategy if it doesn't immediately achieve the projected outcomes?
Is this a proven or new strategy to test? If the latter, does the total investment for new strategies total 20 percent or less of our total projected marketing budget?

t`LORI TURNER-WILSON

**CHECK OUT THE 12 BATTLES™ READER HUB** at marketingtoolsforyou.com for this free resource:

WAR ROOM STRATEGY VETTING WORKSHEET

Success Story

Horizon Industrial Equipment[22], a $20M player in the industrial equipment sector, had reached an inflection point. With the departure of its internal marketing director, the onus fell on David, the VP of sales, to decide the course of action for driving growth. Facing a crossroads, David had to decide between hiring a new in-house marketing director or seeking external expertise. He chose the latter for its promise of a fresh, unbiased strategic vision.

David engaged the RedRover team to deploy our flagship GO Plan service, which blends market research with strategy development, backed by a performance guarantee. Our task was to deploy and distill insights from stakeholder interviews, competitive intelligence, customer transaction analysis, and a customer survey into a marketing plan capable of catapulting Horizon past its growth plateau.

In a dynamic war room strategy debate session, our specialists leveraged their external vantage point to battle assumptions and push boundaries. Based on the insights from the research, we chose a road-show strategy, where a company essentially brings a mini trade-show to its largest prospective customers, a hyper-targeted email campaign, and a referral program for inclusion in Horizon's marketing plan. The outcome was a comprehensive, results-driven marketing strategy tailored to Horizon's unique market position and growth aspirations.

---

[22] Client details have been modified to respect confidentiality.

150

Upon commissioning our team to implement the strategy, Horizon witnessed a 45 percent surge in SQLs (sales qualified leads: leads that have engaged with more advanced company content, such as case studies, pricing details, and product comparisons, and are believed to have buying intent). The execution of our plan yielded an MROI of $7:$1, a testament to the objective, research-led methodology. With David at the helm, guiding both sales and marketing efforts, the company quickly got back on track to meet its growth objectives, demonstrating the clear benefits of having sales and marketing work together toward a common goal.

Cautionary Tale

Vector Engineering Solutions[23], a $22M firm specializing in advanced engineering software, prided itself on a culture of self-reliance. When it came time to revamp its marketing strategy to address stagnating sales, it conducted its market research internally. Confident in its findings, Vector sought RedRover's expertise only to supplement its in-house capabilities, bringing in our SEO, SEM, and social media specialists to assist in its war room strategy debate.

Our specialists dove into the strategy debate with vigor, lending their expertise to a plan that was already in motion. The internal team, led by a marketing director whose zeal for the company's vision was unmatched, presented research that painted an overly optimistic view of the demand for the niche, high-end features of its software—features that the marketing director believed were the most important competitive differentiators.

While our contributions helped to shape a strategy that did yield a modest MROI, the internal research's bias toward these high-end features meant broader market needs were overlooked. For an entire

---

[23] Client details have been modified to respect confidentiality.

year, Vector's strategy chased a narrow segment, missing out on the opportunity to capture a larger market share interested in more practical, user-friendly software solutions.

It wasn't until a year later, when sales figures prompted a re-evaluation, that the bias came to light. The well-intentioned passion of the marketing director had inadvertently skewed the research, proving to be a costly lesson for Vector. The company realized that going forward, an external perspective was crucial from the outset for the objectivity needed in research.

> **START A REVOLUTION: CHALLENGE YOUR TEAM TO MAKE POWERFUL STRATEGIC SHIFTS GROUNDED IN RESEARCH VERSUS TRADITION.**

12 BATTLES™ FRAMEWORK

1 YOU **ACCEPT** THAT YOU DESERVE AND WILL ACHIEVE GUARANTEED MARKETING OUTCOMES.

2 YOU **ACKNOWLEDGE** THAT YOU DON'T REALLY KNOW THY CUSTOMER.

3 YOU **CHAMPION** MARKET RESEARCH AS A DO-OR-DIE INVESTMENT.

4 YOU **EMBRACE** THE POWER OF ATTRIBUTION MODELING AND STOP ACCEPTING BAD DATA.

5 YOU **OWN** AN OPENING IN THE BRANDSCAPE.

6 YOU **TORCH** YOUR EXISTING STRATEGY UNAPOLOGETICALLY IF NEEDED.

7 YOU **ADVOCATE** FOR AN INVESTMENT IN EACH STAGE OF THE CUSTOMER JOURNEY.

8 YOU **CHALLENGE** YOUR TEAM TO MAKE POWERFUL STRATEGIC SHIFTS GROUNDED IN RESEARCH VERSUS TRADITION.

9 YOU **PREACH** THE GOOD WORD OF DISCIPLINED OPTIMIZATION.

10 YOU **COMMIT** TO BUILDING A PAY-FOR-PERFORMANCE TEAM AROUND YOUR STRATEGY; NOT VICE VERSA.

11 YOU **REQUIRE** A POWERFUL MARKETING DASHBOARD AND DOCUMENTED PROCESSES.

12 YOU **INSPIRE** YOUR TEAM TO STAND BEHIND THEIR MROI PROJECTIONS.

BATTLE 9 : YOU **PREACH** THE GOOD WORD OF DISCIPLINED OPTIMIZATION

Battle 9

Battle 9 asks you to preach the good word of disciplined optimization. It's a concept that challenges the status quo and raises the bar—often uncomfortably so.

Most marketing strategies, especially in the B2B space, have historically been set-and-forget. Once a strategy is in place and the campaign is live, many marketers step back, waiting for results to trickle in—and then either stick with the strategy as is for far too long or walk away from it too quickly. This all or nothing approach doesn't work. To guarantee results, marketers must be proactive, iterative, and relentlessly committed to optimization.

> **TO GUARANTEE RESULTS, MARKETERS MUST BE PROACTIVE, ITERATIVE, AND RELENTLESSLY COMMITTED TO OPTIMIZATION.**

Iterative testing involves continually challenging and re-evaluating every campaign element to ensure optimal performance. And that begins with launching each new campaign against a small sample audience to gauge results before heavying up your investment. As Jim Collins puts it in *Great by Choice*, it's the "fire bullets, then cannonballs" approach to market testing.

"Fire bullets, then cannonballs[24]"

This strategy is about the conservation of resources and mitigating risk. No one draws this comparison better than Collins himself:

> *Picture yourself at sea, a hostile ship bearing down on you. You have a limited amount of gunpowder. You take all your gunpowder and use it to fire a big cannonball. The cannonball flies out over the ocean … and misses the target, off by 40 degrees. You turn to your stockpile and discover that you're out of gunpowder. You die.*
>
> *But suppose instead that when you see the ship bearing down, you take a little bit of gunpowder and fire a bullet. It misses by 40 degrees. You make another bullet and fire. It misses by 30 degrees. You make a third bullet and fire, missing by only 10 degrees. The next bullet hits – ping! – the hull of the oncoming ship. Now, you take all the remaining gunpowder and fire a big cannonball along the same line of sight, which sinks the enemy ship. You live.*

In this analogy, "bullets" are low cost, low risk, and low distraction experiments used to test hypotheses and gather data. What con-stitutes low cost certainly varies based on the size of the company. Low risk means that there are minimal consequences if the bullet doesn't hit anything. Low distraction means that there isn't a significant ripple effect across the company in testing the strategy, though it might be high impact for a person or two.

---

[24] Collins, Jim. *Great by Choice*. Harper Business, 2011.

Once you have evidence that your "bullet" is on target—that is, your campaign shows promise—you can then confidently invest in a "cannonball," a larger, more focused, and costly effort designed to hit the target with greater impact.

By applying this approach, companies avoid the common pitfall of investing heavily in untested ideas, which can lead to wasted resources and missed opportunities. Instead, they make informed, strategic decisions that are more likely to result in measurable success. Optimize your marketing strategies before heavying up your investment. This methodical approach to scaling your marketing allows for fine-tuning and adjustments based on real-world feedback, ensuring that when the time comes to launch a full-scale campaign (the "cannonball"), it has a much higher chance of hitting the mark and delivering a strong MROI.

OPTIMIZE YOUR MARKETING STRATEGIES BEFORE HEAVYING UP TO ENSURE THAT WHEN THE TIME COMES TO LAUNCH A FULL-SCALE CAMPAIGN, IT HAS A MUCH HIGHER CHANCE OF HITTING THE MARK.

How to Optimize a Marketing Strategy

For middle-market B2B leaders, optimizing a marketing strategy is a critical process that requires a detailed and measured approach. Effective marketing optimization melds strategic vision with tactical precision. A succinct yet comprehensive approach to optimization focuses on the following high-level assessments:

- **Audience segmentation:** Regularly evaluate and segment your audience to tailor your marketing more precisely.

- **Channel analysis:** Concentrate efforts on channels that yield robust engagement and MROI.

- **Content/creative review:** Ensure your content strategy (both copy and the supporting visuals) evolves with your audience's needs—as demonstrated by their engagement—employing a diverse mix of formats (e.g., written, audio, video, infographics, slide shows, case studies).

- **Performance metrics:** Define and track key metrics that reflect both immediate and long-term success. Seek out both leading and lagging indicators of your performance.

- **Technology stack:** Utilize cutting-edge tools for sharper analytics and streamlined customer engagement. Given the pace at which technological innovations occur in the marketing space, you should regularly re-evaluate your marketing technology (or martech) platforms.

- **Competitive benchmarking:** Keep a finger on the pulse of the competition and adapt to maintain your edge.

Optimization Schedule and Objectives

One of the foundational elements of disciplined optimization is having a structured schedule in place. This ensures consistent checkpoints, regular feedback loops, and timely adjustments. Schedule weekly, monthly, quarterly, and annual optimization meetings with the marketing team to accomplish the following:

- **Weekly check-in:** Review the results of all scheduled A/B tests—whether it be content, graphics, calls to action, or segmentation—and agree upon any needed adjustments to variables scheduled for testing over the coming weeks.

- **Monthly analysis:** Dive into comprehensive analytics, including customer behavior and competitive insights, optimizing campaigns based on those findings.

- **Quarterly strategy session:** Revisit and refine overall marketing strategy, budget allocations, and technology tools based on learnings from the prior quarter.

- **Annual alignment:** Assess the year's performance against strategic objectives and recalibrate the company's marketing vision and budget.

By following this cadence, marketing leaders and CEOs ensure their marketing strategies are not only well-conceived but also rigorously executed and regularly refined.

Weekly Check-In Meeting Agenda

Duration: 30 minutes

1. **Opening and objectives (5 minutes)**
   - Review the agenda.
   - Establish the main goals: To review the performance of the prior week's A/B testing and strategize about any needed changes to the variables to be tested over the coming weeks.

2. **Review of previous week's A/B test results (10 minutes)**
   - Review the result of each variable tested.
   - Determine if a longer test is warranted to gain confidence in the results.

3. **Discuss and agree upon any needed adjustments to variables to test over the next several weeks (10 minutes)**
   - Discuss if the prior week's outcomes raise questions about additional variables worth testing.
   - Adjust the A/B testing calendar accordingly.

4. **Closing and next steps (5 minutes)**
   - Summarize the key decisions and action items.
   - Confirm the date for the next weekly review.

Monthly Optimization Meeting Agenda
Duration: 2 hours

1. **Opening and objectives (5 minutes)**
   - Review the agenda.
   - Establish the main goals: To assess monthly performance and strategize for the coming month.

2. **Review of previous month's goals and KPIs (15 minutes)**
   - Recap the goals set for the past month.
   - Discuss the achievements and shortfalls regarding these goals.

3. **Deep-dive analytics (20 minutes)**
   - Present in-depth analysis of the month's data.
   - Explore customer behavior patterns, website analytics, and campaign results.

4. **Competitive landscape and benchmarking (20 minutes)**
   - Share findings from competitive analysis.
   - Discuss industry benchmarks and your standing.

5. **Customer feedback and market insights (15 minutes)**
   - Review customer feedback collected over the month.
   - Integrate market research insights and trends.

6. **Strategic adjustments (20 minutes)**
   - Based on data and discussions, propose adjustments to strategies.
   - Solicit team input on proposed changes.

7. **Resource and budget allocation (10 minutes)**

- Review the allocation of resources, and budget in light of strategic adjustments.
- Make decisions on reallocation if necessary.

8. **Setting next month's objectives (10 minutes)**
   - Define clear, actionable objectives for the coming month that will ensure overall projected MROI achievement.
   - Assign ownership and establish timelines.

9. **Closing and next steps (5 minutes)**
   - Summarize the key decisions and action items.
   - Confirm the date for the next monthly review.

Quarterly Optimization Meeting Agenda
Duration: Half-day (4 hours)

1. **Opening and objectives (5 minutes)**
   - Outline the meeting's objectives.
   - Emphasize strategic reflection and planning for the upcoming quarter.

2. **Review of previous quarter's performance (30 minutes)**
   - Assess the success against previous quarter's goals.
   - Review key metrics and discuss any insights and learning.

3. **Strategic market analysis (30 minutes)**
   - Present analysis on market trends, customer behavior, and competitive landscape.
   - Discuss potential strategic implications and opportunities.

4. **Channel and campaign deep-dive (30 minutes)**
   - Evaluate the effectiveness of different marketing channels and campaigns.
   - Identify what to scale, maintain, or discontinue.

5. **Technology and process review (20 minutes)**
   - Evaluate current marketing tools and processes.
   - Consider new technologies or improvements to enhance marketing efficiency.

6. **Break (15 minutes)**
   - Short intermission.

7. **Setting new quarterly objectives (45 minutes)**
   - Define S.M.A.R.T. goals for the upcoming quarter.
   - Develop strategies and tactics to achieve these goals.

8. **Content and messaging workshop (45 minutes)**
   - Workshop on aligning content strategy (both copy and visuals) with updated marketing goals.
   - Brainstorm session for creative campaign ideas.

9. **Action plan and roadmap creation (15 minutes)**
   - Outline action items and assign responsibilities.
   - Develop a timeline for implementation and checkpoints.

10. **Closing remarks and feedback (5 minutes)**
    - Recap the meeting's outcomes and next steps.
    - Gather feedback to improve future meetings.

CHECK OUT THE 12 BATTLES™ READER HUB at marketingtoolsforyou.com for this free resource:

OPTIMIZATION MEETING EDITABLE AGENDAS
(INCLUDING AN ANNUAL MEETING AGENDA NOT FOUND IN THE BOOK)

CHECK OUT THE 12 BATTLES™ READER HUB at marketingtoolsforyou.com for this free resource:

OPTIMIZATION MEETING FACILITATION GUIDE

CHECK OUT THE 12 BATTLES™ READER HUB at marketingtoolsforyou.com for this free resource:

MONTHLY OPTIMIZATION MEETING EXCEL WORKSHEET

Championing the Cause

The CEO's Role

While the marketing team is on the frontline of optimization, the CEO plays an equally crucial role:

- **Vision setting:** Establish a clear vision of what optimized marketing looks like for your organization. This clarity will guide efforts across the board.

- **Resource allocation:** Ensure that teams have the necessary tools, technology, and manpower. This might involve reallocating budgets or hiring specialists.

- **Cultural shift:** Drive the cultural change toward accepting and embracing continuous improvement. Celebrate successes, no matter how small, and encourage a mindset of persistent curiosity.

- **Collaboration:** Foster interdepartmental collaboration. An optimized marketing strategy often requires input from sales, customer support, and even product development teams.

Anticipating and Overcoming Challenges

Embarking on a journey of disciplined optimization isn't without its hurdles:

- **Resistance to change:** Long-standing team members might be hesitant to adopt new methods. Address this by emphasizing the long-term benefits and offering adequate training and support.

- **Over-optimization:** In the quest for perfection, there's a risk of becoming too granular and losing sight of the bigger picture. Regularly zoom out to ensure the overall strategy aligns with broader business objectives.

- **Analysis paralysis:** With an influx of data, making decisions can become overwhelming. It's crucial to differentiate between essential metrics and noise.

The Path Forward

Make passive marketing a thing of the past. It's time to champion the relentless pursuit of excellence through disciplined optimization. By understanding its nuances, advocating its principles, and leading the charge in its implementation, leaders can ensure that their marketing efforts aren't just successful, but consistently exceptional.

Battle 9 Research Insights[25]

7% of survey respondents optimize their marketing strategies weekly, which is the best practice. Less than weekly and you're leaving opportunities on the table.

[25] From the "2024 RedRover U.S. Middle-Market B2B Marketing Performance Study," available in the 12 Battles™ Reader Hub at marketingtoolsforyou.com.

36% of survey respondents strongly agree that their marketing team executes a disciplined marketing optimization process and makes strategic adjustments based on performance data. Given how much the average middle-market B2B company invests in marketing, it's curious that this number isn't notably higher. Moreover, these numbers are significantly lower yet in smaller middle-market companies.

Success Story

Precision Industrial Fabricators[26], an $18M family-owned company in the Northeast, recognized that to achieve its expansion goals, especially with a CEO nearing retirement who was heavily involved in bringing in new business through his reputation and natural sales prowess, it needed to evolve beyond its limited marketing approach. Its new venture into strategic ABM (account-based marketing) was aimed at the aerospace sector, where personalized marketing is not just beneficial but necessary due to the industry's complexity.

ABM is a strategy where businesses create hyper-personalized marketing campaigns based on the specific needs, characteristics, and buying patterns of each prospective account. ABM is particularly effective in B2B marketing, as it allows companies to focus on high-value prospects with individually customized messages and offers, leading to higher engagement and conversion rates. It requires sales and marketing to work hand in hand. Generally, an ABM campaign will have eight highly-tailored touchpoints targeting each prospect—a combination of creative, personalized marketing touchpoints combined with value-added sales calls. Why eight? That's how many touches it generally takes before a B2B prospect with a need engages. Anything less than eight is generally considered wasted effort.

---

[26] Client details have been modified to respect confidentiality.

Despite initial skepticism from Precision's owner, Felix, after the early stages of the campaign, we encouraged patience and the importance of completing the full sequence of eight touchpoints. We advised that B2B decision-making cycles can be longer, and it's essential to trust the process. To complement our ABM efforts, we also recommended investing in a dedicated outbound sales specialist with proven expertise in "hunting" to actively pursue leads, as the retiring CEO had been the only source of outbound sales effort to date.

Convinced by our strategy, Felix agreed to continue with the planned eight touchpoints and hired a skilled outbound sales professional. The results were striking: Within the first six months, the targeted outreach to just the initial 50 prospects generated an impressive $2M in new business with the cost to acquire a new prospect dropping notably each of the next four quarters as we continued to optimize the touchpoint plan. This success underscored the power of disciplined marketing optimization and the value of a skilled sales force in executing an ABM strategy effectively.

Cautionary Tale

Clarity Consulting Group[27], a $13M professional services firm, faced a challenge: Its marketing performance lacked transparency and the plan was not yielding the expected returns. The company needed to gain clarity on its MROI and boost its SQLs to support ambitious expansion plans.

Our analysis uncovered that Clarity was unknowingly competing against itself in paid search campaigns, significantly inflating its cost per click. There are a variety of ways this can occur, but, in this case, it was because Clarity had multiple campaigns running simultaneously

---

[27] Client details have been modified to respect confidentiality.

with similar, overlapping keywords. We also identified that a substantial portion of its LinkedIn ad impressions were falling outside its target audience, leading to wasted spend.

Before our optimization efforts, Clarity's LinkedIn campaigns, with a monthly spend of $5000, failed to produce consistent leads. Meanwhile, its Google Ads campaign, with a $15,000 monthly investment, incurred a cost per click that was 152 percent above the industry benchmark, and the cost per conversion was 90 percent higher than the benchmark. These figures highlighted the risks of a "set it and forget it" approach to digital marketing.

> **START A REVOLUTION: PREACH THE GOOD WORD OF DISCIPLINED OPTIMIZATION.**

12 BATTLES™ FRAMEWORK

1 YOU **ACCEPT** THAT YOU DESERVE AND WILL ACHIEVE GUARANTEED MARKETING OUTCOMES.

2 YOU **ACKNOWLEDGE** THAT YOU DON'T REALLY KNOW THY CUSTOMER.

3 YOU **CHAMPION** MARKET RESEARCH AS A DO-OR-DIE INVESTMENT.

4 YOU **EMBRACE** THE POWER OF ATTRIBUTION MODELING AND STOP ACCEPTING BAD DATA.

5 YOU **OWN** AN OPENING IN THE BRANDSCAPE.

6 YOU **TORCH** YOUR EXISTING STRATEGY UNAPOLOGETICALLY IF NEEDED.

7 YOU **ADVOCATE** FOR AN INVESTMENT IN EACH STAGE OF THE CUSTOMER JOURNEY.

8 YOU **CHALLENGE** YOUR TEAM TO MAKE POWERFUL STRATEGIC SHIFTS GROUNDED IN RESEARCH VERSUS TRADITION.

9 YOU **PREACH** THE GOOD WORD OF DISCIPLINED OPTIMIZATION.

10 YOU **COMMIT** TO BUILDING A PAY-FOR-PERFORMANCE TEAM AROUND YOUR STRATEGY; NOT VICE VERSA.

11 YOU **REQUIRE** A POWERFUL MARKETING DASHBOARD AND DOCUMENTED PROCESSES.

12 YOU **INSPIRE** YOUR TEAM TO STAND BEHIND THEIR MROI PROJECTIONS.

BATTLE 10 : YOU **COMMIT** TO BUILDING A PAY-FOR-PERFORMANCE TEAM AROUND YOUR STRATEGY; NOT VICE VERSA

Battle 10

Battle 10 compels you to commit to building a pay-for-performance team around your strategy; not vice versa.

First Things First

When faced with how best to ensure strong execution of your performance-driven marketing strategy, you might wonder: What comes first—the team or the strategy? It's the chicken-or-the-egg debate of the business world, and it's an important question because the best-laid strategy will fail with the wrong execution team.

So, which does come first?

Imagine you build a marketing strategy predominantly based around authority marketing, one where you churn out high-quality written content to establish your brand and leaders as experts in your field. In contrast, imagine that you build a marketing strategy that is predominantly built on trade shows. Content marketing versus event marketing. Would the marketing team you hire differ with each approach?

Certainly. Content marketing and event marketing are two very different games. It takes an entirely different skillset to appeal to an audience with the written word than it does to attract their attention at a large-scale event.

If you were starting from scratch, you'd want to build the strategy and then the team around it. If you already have a marketing team, assess if they hold the precise skills you need for your research-backed marketing strategy, and, if they don't, either invest in their development, have them collaborate with an agency, or make a change.

Relying on the team you have to develop your strategy without external objectivity is risky; with the best intentions, any team naturally develops the strategy that best aligns with its skills, which may differ from the ideal strategy most likely to scale your company. It's human nature. Most companies simply benefit from the objectivity that comes from the outside when putting together a results-guaranteed strategy, no matter if that plan is ultimately executed inside or outside your company.

> **WITH THE ABSOLUTE BEST OF INTENTIONS, ANY TEAM NATURALLY DEVELOPS THE STRATEGY THAT BEST ALIGNS WITH ITS SKILLS, WHICH MAY DIFFER FROM THE IDEAL STRATEGY MOST LIKELY TO SCALE YOUR COMPANY.**

Pitfalls of Generalists in a Specialized World

If you're building an internal execution team, you might be tempted to hire marketing generalists who can do a little bit of everything. But your team's depth of expertise is often the differentiating factor between an effective campaign and a lackluster one. It's why specialization is paramount.

> **YOU MIGHT BE TEMPTED TO HIRE MARKETING GENERALISTS WHO CAN DO A BIT OF EVERYTHING, BUT YOUR TEAM'S DEPTH OF EXPERTISE IS OFTEN THE DIFFERENTIATING FACTOR BETWEEN AN EFFECTIVE CAMPAIGN AND A LACKLUSTER ONE.**

Following is a deeper dive into the three main pitfalls of generalists in such a specialized world:

1. **The depth versus breadth dilemma:** A generalist, by definition, has a broad range of knowledge. They know a little about a lot. This breadth can be an advantage in roles that require multi-tasking across various disciplines such as operations leaders, project managers, account managers, and human resources leaders. However, marketing in today's digital age demands depth. Platforms like Google and Facebook, with their intricate and ever-changing algorithms, require a depth of understanding that only a specialist can offer. A generalist might know how to run a Google Ads campaign, but a specialist would know how to optimize it for maximum MROI. Likewise, when a marketing campaign isn't performing as expected, a generalist might provide a surface-level solution, while a specialist can dig deep, understand the intricacies, and offer a more effective, targeted remedy.

2. **Lack of precision in execution, creating inefficiencies and waste:** Imagine needing a delicate surgery and being operated on by a general practitioner instead of a surgeon specialized in that procedure. The analogy holds in marketing. A generalist might be able to draft content, design graphics, or even run an ad campaign, but the precision and finesse that come with specialization make a significant difference in outcomes. In

marketing, inefficiencies are costly. If a generalist uses the wrong keywords, targets the wrong audience, or even misallocates a budget across platforms, the financial implications can be significant. A specialist ensures that every dollar spent is optimized for maximum return.

3. **Lack of continuous learning in any one specialty:** Marketing is not a static field; it's wildly dynamic, with trends, tools, and tactics changing daily. A generalist, already spread thin across multiple disciplines, may find it challenging to keep up with continuous learning in every needed specialty. In contrast, a specialist, with their focused approach, will find it easier to stay up to date within their domain, ensuring they always employ the best practices, anticipating shifts and preparing strategies to be leveraged in real time.

So, while generalists bring value to a great many situations, the intricate world of marketing demands specialized expertise. In marketing, you need more than just the proverbial hammer to which everything looks like a nail. You need the entire toolbox, with each tool focused on its specific purpose.

If you have marketing generalists on board who have grit, courage, and deep critical-thinking skills—three essential and challenging-to-find traits in your results-guaranteed marketing team—but they lack specialized skills, either invest in their continuous development along one specific specialty or pair them with an agency partner that carries complementary skills.

The In-House Team Versus the Marketing Agency Debate

When you're considering whether you want to build and develop your own in-house team or hire a marketing agency, there's a lot to consider. Both options have their pros and cons.

When I reflect on the hundreds of client marketing plans I've put my hands on over the years, most middle-market B2B companies need the following nine core marketing specialists to handle an optimum marketing strategy:

1. **Marketing director (team leader)**
   - Leadership and team management skills
   - Strategic planning and market research
   - Brand management and campaign planning
   - Budget management and resource allocation
   - Data analysis and performance metrics evaluation

2. **Copywriter**
   - Excellent writing and editing skills
   - Creative thinking and concept development
   - Understanding of target audience and brand voice
   - SEO and digital content optimization
   - Ability to work under deadlines and adapt to various content formats

3. **Art director (graphic designer)**
   - Graphic design and visual communication
   - Proficiency in design software
   - Creative concepting and art direction
   - Brand identity and visual strategy development
   - Team collaboration and project management

4. **PPC specialist**
   - Understanding of SEM
   - PPC campaign management and optimization
   - Keyword research and selection
   - Budget management and MROI analysis
   - Data analysis and A/B testing

5. **SEO specialist**
   - SEO strategies and best practices
   - Keyword research and content optimization
   - Technical SEO and website analysis
   - Link building and online presence management
   - Performance tracking and reporting

6. **Front-end developer**
   - Proficiency in HTML, CSS, and JavaScript
   - Responsive and mobile-first design principles
   - Familiarity with front-end frameworks
   - Cross-browser and cross-platform compatibility
   - Website performance optimization

7. **Social media specialist**
   - Social media strategy and content creation
   - Understanding of social media advertising and platforms
   - Audience engagement and community management
   - Analytics and social media metrics
   - Trend monitoring and brand representation

8. **Digital media buyer**
   - Media planning and buying strategies
   - Negotiation and partnership development
   - Performance analysis and KPI tracking
   - Budget management and cost optimization
   - Understanding of various media channels and their audiences

9. **PR coordinator**
   - Public relations and communications skills
   - Press release writing
   - Event planning and coordination
   - Crisis management and brand reputation
   - Relationship building with media and stakeholders
   - Media pitching (sales) skills

Your payroll for a team of this size—assuming they are all full-time employees for simplicity's sake—will run approximately $630,000, depending on where you are. When you add in benefits, you're looking at roughly $750,000. This doesn't include expenses such as media/advertising, photography/videography costs, your platforms, etc. For a company that needs each of these specialties full time, an internal team has a lot of advantages, namely control and easy collaboration.

> **FOR A COMPANY THAT NEEDS EACH OF THESE SPECIALTIES FULL TIME, AN INTERNAL TEAM HAS A LOT OF ADVANTAGES—NAMELY CONTROL AND EASY COLLABORATION.**

A full-service marketing agency presents a more flexible option for companies that need less than a full-time equivalent of a variety of specialties. Instead of fixed overheads, you can tailor your investment based on your requirements.

> **A FULL-SERVICE MARKETING AGENCY PRESENTS A MORE FLEXIBLE OPTION FOR COMPANIES THAT NEED LESS THAN A FULL-TIME EQUIVALENT OF A VARIETY OF SPECIALTIES AND/OR THE ABILITY TO QUICKLY AND SEAMLESSLY ADAPT STRATEGIES.**

If in Q1 you need more web development work but that need tapers off from Q2 to Q4 when you need more SEO and digital media-buying experience, an agency can allocate only the resources you need in the months you need them, reducing waste. While you pay more per hour than with internal labor, the agency model can adapt seamlessly and often offers a far more cost-effective solution in the end. It also provides the agility to change strategy and the corresponding skills needed for that new strategy without notice or employee ramp. For example, if you hire a team and then realize mid-year that you need to pivot your strategy to take advantage of an opening in the market, you might very well need staffing changes, whereas an agency can quickly and easily make that pivot.

CHECK OUT THE 12 BATTLES™ READER HUB at marketingtoolsforyou.com for this free resource:

AGENCY VS. INTERNAL TEAM COMPARISON GUIDE

Key Questions to Consider

When interviewing marketing firms with the goal of hiring one that will guarantee MROI, marketing leaders or CEOs should ask a series of critical questions to assess the firm's capabilities, approach, and commitment to delivering measurable results:

1. **Do you offer any performance-based pricing or MROI guarantees in your service agreements?** Inquire about its willingness to tie compensation to performance and whether it offers any MROI guarantees in its contracts. While external factors influence marketing outcomes, as many firms will assuredly tell you, if the firm isn't willing to have skin in the game, what kind of partner is it really?

2. **Can you provide case studies or examples of past clients for whom you've delivered a positive MROI?** Request specific examples that demonstrate the firm's ability to generate measurable returns on marketing investments.

3. **What metrics and KPIs do you prioritize when measuring marketing success?** Understand the firm's focus on metrics that matter—such as MROI, incremental sales, or gross profit—to ensure that its metrics align with your goals.

4. **What is your approach to developing a marketing strategy that ensures a strong, predictable MROI?** Seek insights into its strategy development process, including research, planning, and execution, to understand how the firm intends to achieve a strong MROI.

5. **How do you plan to track and report MROI on our marketing campaigns?** Clarify the firm's reporting process, including the frequency of updates and the specific MROI calculations it'll provide—meaning what it includes in its MROI calculation. Ideally, it includes all in-house and firm labor and bases the calculation off of gross profit versus top-line revenue.

6. **What tools and technologies do you use for analytics and performance measurement?** Evaluate the firm's technological capabilities to ensure it has the necessary tools for accurate MROI tracking and analysis.

7. **What strategies do you employ to optimize marketing campaigns and ensure ongoing MROI improvements?** Understand how the firm plans to continuously refine and optimize campaigns to maximize MROI.

8. **How do you handle underperforming campaigns, and what is your process for making necessary adjustments?** Assess its approach to addressing challenges and pivoting when campaigns do not meet MROI expectations. Get a feel for how quickly it adjusts.

9. **How do you stay updated with the latest marketing trends and industry best practices to ensure our campaigns are competitive and MROI-focused?** Assess the firm's commitment to ongoing education and staying current with industry developments.

10. **What is your approach to communication and collaboration with our internal team (if applicable) to ensure alignment with our overall business strategy?** Evaluate its communication practices and willingness to work collaboratively with your in-house team.

11. **Can you provide a roadmap or plan for achieving MROI within a specified timeframe?** You deserve to know how it will arrive at the MROI it stands behind and how long it will take to determine what that projection will be. The firm naturally won't be able to say what that MROI will be until it's conducted research and built your plan, however.

12. **How do you recruit and hire employees who are skilled in delivering predictable outcomes for clients?** Understand the firm's hiring criteria and whether it prioritizes candidates with a track record of achieving results.

13. **What ongoing training and development programs do you have in place to enhance your team's ability to drive MROI for clients?** Assess its commitment to continuous improvement and skill development among its employees because the marketing field is incredibly dynamic. If you don't keep up, you become irrelevant—quickly.

14. **Can you describe your performance evaluation process and how it relates to client outcomes and MROI?** Learn how the firm assesses employee performance and whether it's tied to client success metrics.

15. **Do you have a process for identifying and addressing under-performing employees who aren't achieving client metrics, and how does this impact that client's work?** Understand how the firm handles employees who may not be meeting expectations in terms of client outcomes. You should expect a firm with a higher bar for performance to have both deeper training and coaching programs and higher turnover, as B players won't thrive in this environment.

16. **How do you handle employee promotions and advancement within the firm, and is it linked to their ability to contribute to client MROI?** Assess whether the firm's career advancement opportunities are aligned with a commitment to delivering results.

17. **Can you provide examples of how your employees' contributions have directly led to client success and MROI?** These examples should be top of mind in the right culture.

18. **How do you ensure employees remain motivated to achieve MROI for clients on an ongoing basis?** How does the firm incorporate client outcome wins and losses into its day-to-day activities? How does it inspire its team to deliver?

19. **How does your company culture support a focus on delivering MROI, and what values or principles guide your employees' work?** Understand the cultural aspects of the firm that reinforce a commitment to client outcomes.

20. **Can you share any client testimonials or feedback that highlight the role of your employees in driving MROI for clients?** Request client testimonials or references that specifically mention the contributions of the firm's employees to achieving MROI.

The last nine questions are designed to help you gauge how their internal operations align with their commitment to guaranteed marketing outcomes. In my experience, if the two aren't aligned, your outcomes will suffer.

CHECK OUT THE 12 BATTLES™ READER HUB at marketingtoolsforyou.com for this free resource:

20 QUESTIONS TO ASK AGENCY CONTENDERS

Pay-for-Performance Models

If you already have an internal team in place with the courage and conviction to stand behind their projections and the specialized skills that your marketing plan requires, then make sure they have real skin in the game. This means you must tie their compensation to plan performance.

The best practice is for half or more of their total earnings to come from variable pay tied to the performance of your marketing strategy. A simple yet effective model rewards them for projected MROI achievement. If they achieve 100 percent of the projected MROI, they earn 100 percent of their variable compensation. If they miss the mark by 10 percent, they earn 90 percent. Note that if their base salary is too high, they may lose their fire to fight to deliver that MROI—because it is not easy. CEOs will also want to ensure that the most senior marketing leader is wired to win—meaning they have the inherent drive to win, critical-thinking skills, and problem-solving abilities to lead a team that achieves a guaranteed MROI year-over-year.

**THE BEST PRACTICE IS FOR HALF OR MORE
OF TOTAL EARNINGS TO COME IN VARIABLE PAY
TIED TO THE PERFORMANCE OF YOUR
MARKETING STRATEGY.**

CHECK OUT THE 12 BATTLES™ READER HUB at
marketingtoolsforyou.com for this free resource:

INTERNAL PAY-FOR-PERFORMANCE MODELS

If you don't have an internal team, then consider an agency partnership. Ideally, the same agency partner that develops your strategy should also execute it, which helps avoid the blame game if things go sideways. This is not required if expectations of the agency hired to execute your strategy are abundantly clear and documented, however. Like your internal team, your agency partner must also have skin in the game with their fees tied, ideally, to projected MROI goals. If you have both an internal team and an agency relationship, you want both team's compensation tied to the same outcomes so that they all win or lose together. The company is more likely to win as a result.

Battle 10 Research Insights[28]

28% of survey respondents built their marketing strategy first and then built the marketing team needed to execute that strategy. This is ideal, but not the norm. Forty-six percent,

---

[28] From the "2024 RedRover U.S. Middle-Market B2B Marketing Performance Study," available in the 12 Battles™ Reader Hub at marketingtoolsforyou.com.

the most common response, built both at the same time. This often means they hired a marketing leader to build their strategy. Because the most well-intended teams build strategies that align with their unique skills as compared to the strategy most likely to win for your company, the best practice is to build the strategy first and then recruit the specialized team or agency most experienced at delivering on the elements of your marketing plan.

39% of survey respondents strongly agree that their team is highly aligned with their marketing strategy. The odds are slim that you'll maximize your marketing opportunities when your strategy and team are out of alignment.

63% of survey respondents use a marketing agency exclusively or in combination with their internal team to execute their marketing plan. Only 37 percent use an internal team alone.

61% of respondents who use an internal team alone do so to keep their costs low. Fifty-three percent use an internal team for greater control.

18% of respondents that use an agency only (no internal team) strongly agree that a significant portion of their marketing team's total compensation is tied to their performance. That number increases to 32 percent for respondents using an agency and internal team, and drops to just 17 percent for those using an internal team only. This is the direction that marketing is headed and an opportunity for you to level up your expectations and performance—whether your team is internal, external, or both.

23% of survey respondents earn a $3:$1 to $4:$1 MROI with leadership generally satisfied but not highly satisfied with that result. Most work with an agency partner to generate that performance. Satisfaction rises when the agency guarantees MROI, yet most B2B companies are not yet partnering with an agency that offers a performance guarantee of any kind.

39% of survey respondents strongly agree that they are more likely to partner with an agency that offers a guaranteed return on overall marketing investment. Forty-four percent of respondents agree with this statement.

23% of survey respondents say that when selecting their next agency partner, the top factor driving that choice is accountability for performance, followed by a performance/results/MROI guarantee.

Success Story

Skyward Bound[29], a $28M national online pilot training provider, realized the need for an enhanced social media strategy. Its social media efforts, led by an internal marketing generalist, Beth, were brand-consistent yet failed to make a significant impact—engagement was sparse, and tracking from content to conversion was non-existent.

CEO and founder, Sylvia, driven to see different results, was ready for change. Our first action was to implement robust tracking, enabling us to follow user engagement from initial contact to final conversion. Concurrently, we embarked on extensive market research, which gave us an abundance of clarity into what types of messaging and visuals pilots were likely to respond to. The type of content that pilots said they would most respond to was:

- **Real-life success:** Featuring testimonials and case studies of pilots who have successfully completed online recertification training, which adds credibility and relatability.

---

[29] Client details have been modified to respect confidentiality.

- **Engaging visuals:** High-quality images and videos of aircraft, cockpit views, and detailed infographics on aviation topics to capture their attention and provide value.

- **Interactive content:** Quizzes and polls about aviation topics to engage them in a conversational way, along with flight simulation clips that showcase the practical aspects of the training.

- **Educational snippets:** Best practices for navigating the complex world of aviation regulations, highlighting the ease of staying compliant through Skyward Bound's courses.

- **User-generated content:** Encouraging users to share their flying experiences and learning journeys, which fosters a sense of community and peer-to-peer learning.

- **Inspirational quotes and stories:** Motivational content from renowned aviators and success stories in the field.

Assessing Beth's workplace traits through a psychometric employee assessment tool, we discovered a mismatch between her abilities and the demands of content production. Her skills were more suited for a role overseeing content logistics and analytics. Our agency filled the content production gap, while Beth excelled in managing organic post logistics and weekly reporting.

By realigning roles and adjusting the focus of content and visuals to align with pilot needs and wants, we achieved a dramatic decrease in social media advertising spend, cutting costs by 46 percent to $126,000 for the year, without compromising on results. In fact, profits from sales attributable to social media saw a 69 percent increase year-over-year.

Sylvia's willingness to build a team tailored to an innovative strategy, complemented by our objective third-party insights, laid the groundwork for a resounding success story in social media marketing.

Cautionary Tale

Vector Industrial Systems[30], an $8M industrial machinery and equipment supplier targeting the automotive manufacturing vertical, had a long history of struggling to scale its sales efforts. Its CEO, Max, was on the hunt for a new solution—either a new sales strategy or marketing lead generation to support the sales team.

We began our work together by kicking off a robust research protocol where we spent quite a bit of time talking to Vector's customers. We learned through these in-person interviews that no amount of marketing lead generation alone would drive them to consider a supplier in Vector's particular industry. The customers needed a personal relationship with a sales representative in order to feel comfortable making a purchase.

What Vector needed was an ABM strategy. As a reminder, ABM (account-based marketing) is a strategy where businesses create hyper-personalized marketing campaigns comprised of a combination of sales and marketing touchpoints—usually eight—in order to get the typical prospect to engage. When we presented the strategy to Max, we voiced concern that David, the only sales representative, while extremely loyal to the company, didn't appear to be wired to hunt. Max assured us that with ABM in his toolbelt, David would be up for the challenge.

The initial implementation of ABM saw David's meeting booking rates soar to 28 percent, a substantial increase from his previous rate of below 5 percent. Yet over time, the intensity of the outreach required began to weigh on David, prompting concerns about the sustainability

[30] Client details have been modified to respect confidentiality.

of the effort. In an attempt to address this, Max streamlined the ABM process from eight to just three touchpoints, aiming to tailor the strategy more closely to his team's capabilities. This adjustment, however, had an immediate and adverse effect, with the meeting booking rate plunging back to around the initial 5 percent.

This case study exemplifies the delicate balance required between a robust marketing strategy and the operational capacity of a sales team and demonstrates the risks involved in building your strategy around your team—whether it be your marketing or sales team.

START A REVOLUTION: COMMIT TO BUILDING A PAY-FOR-PERFORMANCE TEAM AROUND YOUR STRATEGY; NOT VICE VERSA.

---

12 BATTLES™ FRAMEWORK

1 YOU **ACCEPT** THAT YOU DESERVE AND WILL ACHIEVE GUARANTEED MARKETING OUTCOMES.

2 YOU **ACKNOWLEDGE** THAT YOU DON'T REALLY KNOW THY CUSTOMER.

3 YOU **CHAMPION** MARKET RESEARCH AS A DO-OR-DIE INVESTMENT.

4 YOU **EMBRACE** THE POWER OF ATTRIBUTION MODELING AND STOP ACCEPTING BAD DATA.

5 YOU **OWN** AN OPENING IN THE BRANDSCAPE.

6 YOU **TORCH** YOUR EXISTING STRATEGY UNAPOLOGETICALLY IF NEEDED.

7 YOU **ADVOCATE** FOR AN INVESTMENT IN EACH STAGE OF THE CUSTOMER JOURNEY.

8 YOU **CHALLENGE** YOUR TEAM TO MAKE POWERFUL STRATEGIC SHIFTS GROUNDED IN RESEARCH VERSUS TRADITION.

9 YOU **PREACH** THE GOOD WORD OF DISCIPLINED OPTIMIZATION.

10 YOU **COMMIT** TO BUILDING A PAY-FOR-PERFORMANCE TEAM AROUND YOUR STRATEGY; NOT VICE VERSA.

11 YOU **REQUIRE** A POWERFUL MARKETING DASHBOARD AND DOCUMENTED PROCESSES.

12 YOU **INSPIRE** YOUR TEAM TO STAND BEHIND THEIR MROI PROJECTIONS.

BATTLE 11 : YOU **REQUIRE** A
POWERFUL MARKETING DASHBOARD
AND DOCUMENTED PROCESSESS

Battle 11

Battle 11 requires a powerful marketing dashboard and documented processes.

The objective of this battle is crystal clear: To empower you with the insights and metrics necessary to make confident and ROI-driven marketing decisions.

> **A MARKETING DASHBOARD EMPOWERS YOU WITH THE INSIGHTS AND METRICS TO MAKE CONFIDENT AND ROI-DRIVEN MARKETING DECISIONS.**

Marketing Dashboard Necessities

MROI
The cornerstone of your marketing dashboard is MROI. It's the North Star, the guiding light that illuminates the path to profitability. In

Battle 4, I reviewed how to properly calculate MROI—including too often forgotten costs impacting your returns. With MROI firmly in place, let's move on to three additional pivotal metrics: LTV, CAC, and the all-important LTV:CAC ratio.

LTV

LTV is a measure of the average financial worth of each customer over their entire engagement with your business. LTV considers both the longevity of the customer relationship and the profitability it generates. Following is the formula.

LTV = (Average annual gross profit per customer) x (Average lifespan of a customer in years)

Let's break it down with a sample calculation:

- Average annual gross profit last year: $4,937,411
- Total number of customers last year: 150
- Average annual gross profit per customer: $4,937,411/150 = $32,916
- Average lifespan of a customer: 1.5 years
- LTV = $32,916 x 1.5 = $49,374 per customer

This calculation reveals that, on average, each customer contributes more than $49,000 in gross profit over their lifetime with your company. Knowing this value empowers you to make strategic decisions regarding your marketing investments. What would you be willing to invest if you knew the average lifetime gross profit per new customer was nearly $50,000?

CHECK OUT THE 12 BATTLES™ READER HUB at **marketingtoolsforyou.com** for this free resource:

GUIDE FOR CALCULATING AVERAGE CUSTOMER LIFESPAN

CAC

CAC represents the expense incurred to acquire a new customer. It is a crucial metric for evaluating the efficiency and cost-effectiveness of your marketing efforts. The following formula for determining the CAC for all marketing spend works like the formula for the more limited purpose of determining the CAC for a given marketing channel as discussed in Battle 4.

Marketing costs / Number of new customers

Let's break it down with a sample calculation:

- Marketing costs last year (including salaries, benefits, agency fees, ad spend): $338,773
- Number of new customers last year: 75
- CAC = $338,773/75 = $4,516 per new customer

This calculation reveals that it is costing you $4,516 for every new customer you acquire. Depending upon the LTV of a new customer, this might be wonderful or tragic.

CHECK OUT THE 12 BATTLES™ READER HUB at marketingtoolsforyou.com for this free resource:

GUIDE FOR CALCULATING ACCURATE CAC METRIC

The LTV:CAC Ratio

With both LTV and CAC at your disposal, you can calculate the LTV:CAC ratio, a key indicator of your marketing efficiency. This powerful ratio measures the relationship between the lifetime value of a customer and the cost of acquiring that customer.

LTV/CAC

Let's break it down with a sample calculation using the numbers in the preceding two calculations:

- LTV: $49,374
- CAC: $4,516
- LTV:CAC = $49,374/$4,516 = 10.93

An LTV:CAC ratio of 10.93 indicates that for every $1 spent on customer acquisition, your company earns approximately $10.93 in gross profit over the lifetime of that customer. This metric is invaluable for assessing the overall health of your marketing strategy.

The Power of the LTV:CAC Ratio

The LTV:CAC ratio serves as a compass for your marketing decisions. Here's how to interpret it:

- **A ratio below 1:** This suggests that your CAC exceeds the LTV generated by each customer. It's a warning sign that requires attention and strategy adjustments. This could involve shifting focus to high-converting platforms or refining your target audience to ensure your marketing efforts are reaching the most receptive potential customers. You might choose to shift to more cost-effective, organic marketing strategies like content marketing and SEO. By producing high-quality, relevant content that improves your search rankings, you can attract and engage potential customers at a lower cost than traditional paid advertising. Though this is a longer game, you'll improve your CAC over time. You could also increase the LTV of existing customers through loyalty programs, upselling strategies, or offering incentives for repeat purchases. By increasing the average customer lifespan with your company through improved customer service, you raise the LTV without necessarily increasing acquisition costs.

- **A ratio of 1:** While breaking even is not inherently bad, particularly in the early days of a new marketing strategy when you're building your campaigns and website, it is clearly not where you want to be long term. You are not running a nonprofit.

- **A ratio above 1:** A ratio greater than 1 signifies that your marketing investments are paying off. It suggests that, over time, each customer is generating more profit than it costs to acquire them. This is the sweet spot. Anything over 1 is good and worthy of added investment. Your goal is to increase this number over time.

The LTV:CAC ratio, when kept above 1, ensures that your marketing efforts consistently yield positive returns. It is a critical component of your marketing dashboard, aligning your strategy with the ultimate goal of guaranteed MROI.

Putting It All Together
The four key metrics—MROI, LTV, CAC, and LTV:CAC—form the cornerstone of your marketing dashboard. These metrics not only provide a high-level view of your marketing strategy's effectiveness but also set the stage for more granular analysis at the channel and campaign levels. This deeper dive into the data is critical for understanding the nuances of each campaign and its contribution to your overall marketing goals.

Take, for instance, a multi-channel campaign aimed at promoting a specific product. Your marketing efforts might span across diverse platforms such as LinkedIn, email, PPC, and retargeting ads. For a comprehensive assessment, your dashboard should display the following aggregate campaign metrics:

- MQLs
- SQLs
- MROI
- LTV:CAC

In addition, you must break down these same metrics by individual channel.

It's crucial to remember that you can't evaluate the performance of a single channel in isolation when considering optimizations or cuts in your strategy. Each channel should be considered within the broader context of its role in the customer journey and how it fits into your specific attribution model. This holistic view is essential for making informed decisions that truly enhance your marketing effectiveness.

By adopting this multi-layered approach, your marketing dashboard transforms into a powerful tool, providing both a bird's-eye view and a microscopic analysis of your marketing strategies. It becomes easier to identify which channels are driving the most value, where to allocate resources for maximum impact, and how to tweak your strategies for better performance.

Following is a marketing dashboard layout showing just the aggregate metrics to help visualize this concept. Detailed campaign and channel metrics would be visible by clicking deeper into the dashboard. This sample serves as a practical framework to guide you in creating a dashboard tailored to your organization's needs, one that not only tracks KPIs but also offers actionable insights for strategic decision making.

EXECUTIVE OVERVIEW
MARKETING DASHBOARD
MROI, LEAD VOLUME & LTV:CAC (TRAILING 3 MONTHS)

JAN 1 – JAN 31 ⌄

MROI	LTV	Spend (Thousands)	Revenue (Thousands)	New Sales (#)	CAC (trailing 3)
614%	**$130,000**	**$112**	**$800**	**95**	**$1179**
↑ 39.4%	0.0%	↑ 0.9%	↑ 33.3%	↑ 82.7%	↓ -44.8%

HISTORICAL KEY METRICS (TRAILING 3 MONTHS)							
DATE ⌄	MROI	LTV	SPEND	REVENUE	NEW SALES (#)	CAC	LTV : CAC
JAN	614%	$130,000	$112,000	$800,000	95	$1,179	110.27:1
DEC	441%	$130,000	$111,000	$600,000	52	$2,135	60.9:1
NOV	221%	$130,000	$109,000	$350,000	34	$3,206	40.55:1

MONTHLY TRENDS
CAC/Spend/Revenue in Thousands

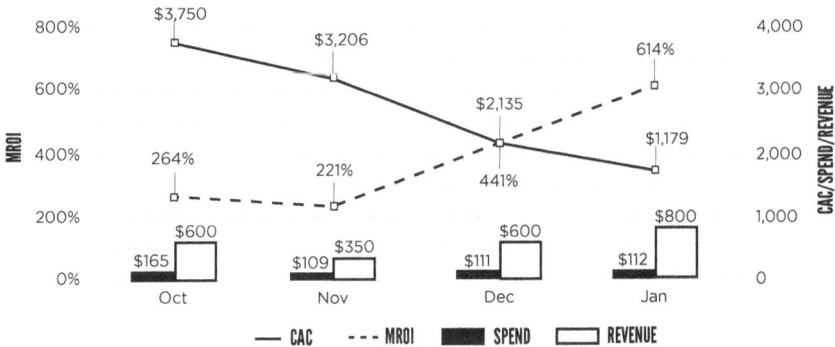

Legend: —— CAC - - - MROI ▬ SPEND ▭ REVENUE

DATE ⌄	NOTES
JAN	**Summary:** The strategic approach to marketing and customer acquisition has yielded remarkable results, significantly enhancing company growth and profitability. Continuing to refine these strategies, while exploring new opportunities for expansion and improvement, will be key to sustaining this positive trajectory.
	Exceptional Improvement in MROI: MROI has seen a tremendous upward trend, demonstrating the marketing strategies and execution are highly effective, maximizing the return on every dollar spent.
	Decreasing CAC: The continuous decrease in CAC while scaling revenue indicates strong optimization of marketing strategies, as marketing efforts are producing higher quality leads at a lower cost.
	Next Steps: (1) Given the dramatic improvements in MROI and LTV:CAC ratios, continue to reallocate budget to the most successful marketing channels and strategies. (2) Given the efficiency of the current campaigns, begin experimenting with new markets and segments by implementing test and pivot strategies.

You can choose from many software platform options to create your own powerful marketing dashboard.

CHECK OUT THE 12 BATTLES™ READER HUB at marketingtoolsforyou.com for this free resource:

TOP DASHBOARD PLATFORMS

Documented Processes

With your dashboard in place, ensuring you are monitoring the metrics that matter most, the last step in your marketing results-guaranteed journey is to document the processes that deliver your outcomes—whether good or bad. That's right; set the expectation that every process of consequence is documented by your marketing team no matter its current outcome. Why? Because you need to understand with clarity exactly what processes your marketing employees consistently follow before you'll be able to work with the team to improve those processes. The holy grail of marketing is to create a truly scalable and repeatable marketing plan. Everything you've learned so far in this book gets you to scalable strategies, but *repeatable* requires documented processes that are followed by all. You should be able to place any skilled specialist into a seat on your marketing team and, if they follow your processes, have a similar result to others executing that same process.

> THE HOLY GRAIL OF MARKETING IS TO CREATE A TRULY SCALABLE AND REPEATABLE MARKETING PLAN SO THAT ANY TWO REASONABLY SKILLED SPECIALISTS FOLLOWING YOUR PROCESSES WOULD HAVE A SIMILAR RESULT.

The same holds true for your agency. Before selecting an agency partner, ask agency leadership how well their team documents its marketing operational practices, and how they hold their team accountable to following those processes. They are unlikely to share the actual SOPs (standard operating procedures) with you, however, as they are likely a proprietary part of the agency's model. Instead, just ask for a simple list of the names of the agency's documented processes, including detail on how often those processes are covered in team training and how leadership holds its team accountable to following those processes.

Following are a few of the marketing processes you should consider documenting:

- **Market research:**
  - Objective setting
  - Data collection methods (surveys, focus groups, online tools)
  - Frequency of ongoing research
  - Data analysis and reporting
  - Feedback loops for product or service improvement

- **Content creation:**
  - Topic ideation
  - Content format determination (blog, video, podcast, etc.)
  - Writing, editing, and approval processes
  - Publishing and promotion

- **Social media management:**
  - Platform selection and optimization
  - Content scheduling
  - Engagement guidelines (responding to comments, DMs) by platform
  - Hashtag protocols by platform
  - Crisis management

- **Email marketing:**
  - List segmentation and management
  - Email design and copywriting guidelines
  - Scheduling and frequency
  - A/B testing procedures
  - Metrics tracking and analysis
  - Campaign monitoring and optimization

- **SEO:**
  - Keyword research
  - On-page optimization (meta tags, content, images)
  - Off-page optimization (backlinking strategies)
  - Reporting and metrics analysis

- **Paid advertising:**
  - Campaign objective setting
  - Target audience segmentation
  - Ad design and copywriting
  - Budget allocation and bidding strategies
  - A/B testing procedures
  - Campaign monitoring and optimization

- **Event marketing:**
  - Event planning and logistics
  - Promotion and ticket sales
  - On-site event management
  - Post-event feedback and analysis

- **PR and media relations:**
  - Press release creation and distribution
  - Media list management
  - Crisis communication
  - Tracking media mentions and coverage

- **Analytics and reporting:**
  - Selection of KPIs
  - Data collection methods and tools
  - Data analysis and interpretation
  - Reporting formats and frequency

- **Brand guidelines:**
  - Logo usage
  - Color palette
  - Typography
  - Tone of voice and messaging

- **Affiliate and influencer marketing:**
  - Partner selection criteria
  - Contract negotiations and terms
  - Campaign tracking and payment terms

- **Lead generation and nurturing:**
  - Target audience profiling
  - Lead magnet creation
  - Landing page design and optimization
  - Lead scoring and follow-up

- **Product launches:**
  - Market analysis and positioning
  - Pre-launch promotional strategies
  - Launch day logistics
  - Post-launch feedback collection

- **Customer feedback and reviews:**
  - Collection methods (surveys, online reviews)
  - Review response guidelines
  - Repurposing positive reviews in marketing efforts
  - Feedback integration into product/service improvements

- **Website optimization:**
  - Periodic website audits (quarterly, bi-annually, etc.)
  - Regular monitoring for broken links
  - Usability testing schedules
  - Mobile responsiveness checks
  - Site speed and performance evaluations

- **CRO (conversion rate optimization):**
  - A/B testing schedules for landing pages, CTAs, and other key elements
  - Funnel analysis and drop-off point assessments
  - Regularly scheduled reviews of analytics to identify areas of improvement

When developing an SOP for any of these processes, it's essential to provide detailed step-by-step instructions, define responsibilities for each task, specify tools or software to be used, and set timelines where appropriate. Regularly reviewing and updating SOPs—ideally quarterly—to align with the latest best practices, tools, and market conditions is equally important.

CHECK OUT THE 12 BATTLES™ READER HUB at marketingtoolsforyou.com for this free resource:

MARKETING SOP TEMPLATE

The Journey Ahead

I've laid the groundwork for your marketing dashboard, incorporating MROI, LTV, CAC, and the LTV:CAC ratio at the company, campaign, and channel levels. These metrics offer a comprehensive view of your marketing performance and financial health. By integrating them into your dashboard, you empower yourself and your team to make data-driven decisions, allocate resources wisely, and ensure a path toward guaranteed MROI.

Imagine your budget meetings taking on a whole new dimension. Instead of simply requesting budgets, the marketing team presents estimated MROI figures, providing a clear justification for their requests with accurate, relevant historical performance. Your marketing dashboard becomes a dynamic tool that not only assesses past performance but also guides future strategies.

Pair this measurement with documented processes that are followed by all, and you are well on your way to a truly scalable and repeatable marketing strategy—one that will drive consistent, even guaranteed, outcomes ... one that allows you to better predict your growth and prepare for it ... one that notably drives up your company's valuation.

In our data-driven world, the ability to track, analyze, and optimize marketing investments is paramount. By focusing on guaranteed MROI and the ability to replicate it no matter who is on your team, you align your marketing strategy with a singular purpose: Driving profitability and sustainable growth.

Each metric, each calculation, and each data point brings you closer to mastering the science of MROI. With your marketing dashboard as your compass, you're not just navigating the terrain, you're confidently charting the course to guaranteed marketing success.

Battle 11 Research Insights[31]

26% of survey respondents strongly agree that their marketing team produces a marketing dashboard (or reporting) that's accurate and actionable.

33% indicate that they receive these reports weekly, followed by 26 percent that receive them monthly.

23% of respondents earn a $3:$1 or $4:$1 MROI, followed by 19 percent that earn a $1:$1 or $2:$1 MROI. MROI performance increases with budget and company size.

44% of survey respondents say the marketing reporting they receive makes it easy to make decisions. Forty percent say it gives them confidence in how their marketing plan is performing. Thirty-eight percent say it clearly shows which channels are performing; 36 percent indicate it includes next steps to improve or continue; and 30 percent say their reports are summarized into a dashboard that's available real-time.

29% of respondents indicate that their marketing reporting is a tool they use to drive company growth.

16% say they leverage attribution modeling in their marketing reporting, which is a massive opportunity to improve informed decision making and outcomes.

$4,537 is the average CAC among middle-market B2B survey respondents. At an average lifetime of five years per customer and an average annual spend of $59,704, the average customer LTV is $298,520. Thus, the LTV:CAC ratio is 66, which means that every $1 spent to acquire a customer

---

[31] From the "2024 RedRover U.S. Middle-Market B2B Marketing Performance Study," available in the 12 Battles™ Reader Hub at marketingtoolsforyou.com.

generates \$66 in return. It's important to keep in mind that this number is notably inflated. Most survey respondents indicated they omit from their CAC calculations marketing salaries, marketing platforms, and the cost of their agency relationship, which is not the best practice.

Success Story

Optima Solutions[32], a \$26M software development company, faced a critical challenge. The CEO, Tammie, knew that the marketing metrics being reported were not reliable and that she didn't have the internal expertise on her team to solve the issue. She sought out RedRover for an external vantage point and to gain a clear understanding of the company's marketing performance.

The RedRover team identified that customer interactions on different channels—such as social media, email campaigns, and online advertising—were being tracked in isolation without any interconnection. This siloed approach led to significant challenges in accurately attributing customer conversions to specific marketing efforts. It was unclear which channels were effectively contributing to customer engagement and which were not, making it difficult for Optima to allocate its marketing resources efficiently and hindering its ability to tailor strategies to customer behaviors and preferences.

The implications of these integration issues were far-reaching. First, it led to a misinterpretation of the effectiveness of various marketing channels, resulting in the misallocation of marketing budgets and efforts. Second, without a clear understanding of the customer journey, Optima was missing out on critical insights that could drive more personalized and effective marketing campaigns. Finally, these data integrity issues meant that Optima's marketing strategies were not as responsive or adaptive to changing market conditions and

---

[32] Client details have been modified to respect confidentiality.

customer needs as they could be. By addressing these integration challenges and creating a unified view of its marketing data via an accurate and actionable marketing dashboard, Optima was able to make more informed decisions.

The result of this partnership was a substantial 72 percent increase in MROI within six months due to the optimizations now obvious thanks to the accuracy of the data.

Cautionary Tale

In the environmental consulting services space, data-driven decision making is not merely an advantage but a necessity. This was a lesson learned the hard way by EcoSphere[33], a $10M company specializing in environmental compliance and sustainable operations. Its passionate and beloved CEO, Stanley, relied on intuition over data, leading to costly consequences.

Despite a history of profitable and steady growth, the company faced a pivotal moment (around 2017) when the industry began to shift dramatically. The rise of digital marketing and data analytics offered a golden opportunity to harness data for strategic decisions. The company's marketing dashboard, rich with insights on customer behavior, acquisition costs, and campaign effectiveness, was signaling a clear need to adapt. However, Stanley chose to lean on his instincts. He dismissed the dashboard's clear warnings about declining engagement in key demographics and increasing acquisition costs, in addition to strong empirical evidence about a substantial new market opportunity ripe for the picking.

The practical fallout of this aversion to data was severe with financial performance waning notably. Eager to refresh the company's image

---

[33] Client details have been modified to respect confidentiality.

as a strategy for improving performance, Stanley redirected resources from lead generation to an extensive rebranding initiative. This process, however, turned into an 18-month ordeal without any substantial entry into new markets. The dashboard had indicated a ripe market for expansion and hinted at effective channels for lead generation, but these insights went unheeded. This strategic misstep was compounded by emerging internal leadership struggles, leading to a complete halt of all marketing activities for an additional 9 months. The absence of a robust marketing engine, coupled with Stanley's dismissal of consumer behavior trends and marketing metrics, left the company unprepared for market shifts. This resulted in a staggering opportunity loss estimated at nearly $3M in revenue over two years—a sum that could have been a catalyst for growth and innovation.

This case serves as a cautionary tale for businesses navigating the digital age. It underscores the peril of sidelining empirical clarity offered by a marketing dashboard in favor of intuition alone. Ultimately, EcoSphere's journey stands as a stark example of the cost of ignoring data-driven insights.

> **START A REVOLUTION: REQUIRE A POWERFUL MARKETING DASHBOARD AND DOCUMENTED PROCESSES.**

12 BATTLES™ FRAMEWORK

1 YOU **ACCEPT** THAT YOU DESERVE AND WILL ACHIEVE GUARANTEED MARKETING OUTCOMES.

2 YOU **ACKNOWLEDGE** THAT YOU DON'T REALLY KNOW THY CUSTOMER.

3 YOU **CHAMPION** MARKET RESEARCH AS A DO-OR-DIE INVESTMENT.

4 YOU **EMBRACE** THE POWER OF ATTRIBUTION MODELING AND STOP ACCEPTING BAD DATA.

5 YOU **OWN** AN OPENING IN THE BRANDSCAPE.

6 YOU **TORCH** YOUR EXISTING STRATEGY UNAPOLOGETICALLY IF NEEDED.

7 YOU **ADVOCATE** FOR AN INVESTMENT IN EACH STAGE OF THE CUSTOMER JOURNEY.

8 YOU **CHALLENGE** YOUR TEAM TO MAKE POWERFUL STRATEGIC SHIFTS GROUNDED IN RESEARCH VERSUS TRADITION.

9 YOU **PREACH** THE GOOD WORD OF DISCIPLINED OPTIMIZATION.

10 YOU **COMMIT** TO BUILDING A PAY-FOR-PERFORMANCE TEAM AROUND YOUR STRATEGY; NOT VICE VERSA.

11 YOU **REQUIRE** A POWERFUL MARKETING DASHBOARD AND DOCUMENTED PROCESSES.

12 YOU **INSPIRE** YOUR TEAM TO STAND BEHIND THEIR MROI PROJECTIONS.

BATTLE 12 : YOU **INSPIRE** YOUR TEAM TO STAND BEHIND THEIR MROI PROJECTIONS

Battle 12

Battle 12 counts on you to inspire your team to establish and stand behind their MROI and outcome projections.

From the moment you decided that you deserved guaranteed MROI, you embarked on a path less trodden. Every step you've taken so far has been about aligning, optimizing, and preparing. Now, it's time for the next monumental shift in perspective. This revolution calls for the kind of inspiration that drives teams to not only make bold MROI projections but to passionately stand behind them.

Performance Projections

At the start of each year, your internal or external team should establish clear projections for the performance of your overall marketing plan to include:

1. MROI

2. MQLs
3. SQLs
4. Revenue generated from marketing leads
5. Gross profit generated from these leads

Accurately projecting the performance of your marketing strategies is a process combining historical analysis, industry benchmarks, and, where needed, strategic testing—all of which is vetted against your market research insights.

Existing Strategy Optimization Projections

If you have a solid track record of marketing performance, where 80 percent of the strategies in your plan for the upcoming year have a proven track record of measurable outcomes, you have a nice foundation for accurate projections. Start with the incremental revenue that those strategies generated in the prior year, and then examine the optimizations to these strategies that you have planned for the coming year. Conservatively estimate the boost in performance that you believe these optimizations will drive based on your research findings. For example, consider an optimization to your LinkedIn strategy that delivered $750,000 in incremental revenue last year. Suppose you plan to enhance this strategy by refining your targeting criteria and improving ad creative based on customer feedback and engagement data. If these optimizations are projected to improve performance by 15 percent, based on past trends and enhanced engagement rates observed in pilot tests, you could conservatively estimate the strategy to deliver approximately $862,500 in incremental revenue this year.

New Strategy Projections Based on Historical Performance

Next, look at your new strategies through the lens of your market research and your past channel and sales team performance. For example, let's assume that you are a SaaS company, and 60 percent of your customers said in your survey that they highly value 24/7 tech support. This VIP service is the reason they spend $50,000 more a year with your competitor who offers it, but they are not highly satisfied with your competitor's service levels. They are, however, highly satisfied with yours.

You currently only offer 24/7 tech support to select VIP customers; now, based on this survey data, you plan to roll it out to all customers for $25,000 a year. Your primary channel for this roll out will be a weekly email campaign across all of the first quarter. You conservatively estimate that just 10 percent, compared to the 60 percent who indicated interest in the survey, of your 10,000 customers will be interested in this VIP tech support add-on service and request a sales meeting as a result, which is in line with your historical email conversion rates. Of those 10 percent that book meetings, 60 percent will show up to them, and 10 percent will buy, which aligns with the current close rate your team enjoys when upselling current clients.

In this scenario, with 10 percent of the 10,000 customers showing interest in the VIP service and booking meetings, you're looking at 1,000 customers. Assuming a 60 percent show-up rate, about 600 will attend the meetings. With a purchase rate of 10 percent, this means 60 customers will finalize their purchase. Given that each service is valued at $25,000 per year, the projected incremental revenue from this campaign totals $1,500,000 a year.

New Strategy Projections Based on Industry Benchmarks

If you don't have the prior performance data needed to accurately project your future marketing performance, you can turn to industry benchmarks. These often can be found through industry associations or market research firms. They provide a valuable reference point for what's achievable in your sector. For instance, a B2B company in a relatively stable industry like manufacturing might find that industry benchmarks show a consistent pattern of customer engagement and sales cycles, while a company in a more dynamic field like tech startups might see greater fluctuations in these industry metrics and find them less useful.

New Strategy Projections Based on Small-Scale Testing

If you are exploring newer strategies or lack sufficient historical data that you trust, and industry benchmarks prove elusive, take inspiration from Jim Collins: "Fire bullets, then cannonballs." Start with small-scale tests to gauge effectiveness before fully committing to and investing in an unproven strategy. The insights gained here will inform your projections, allowing for more accurate forecasting. Note that it may take up to one year to get to predictable outcome projections.

Establish a Margin of Error

Marketing is both art and science, and customers are fickle. So, while you've done all of your research and due diligence, you must still allow for unforeseen market fluctuations, like a large new competitor entering the market that was unknown to you at the time the projections were set. You'll want to establish this margin of error based on the turbulence of your industry. For a relatively stable industry like commercial real estate, the margin of error might be narrow, reflecting the generally predictable nature of the market. Consider a margin of error of 5 to 10 percent for these types of stable industries. In contrast, for a dynamic industry like renewable energy, where market conditions can change rapidly and often unpredictably, a wider margin of error, such as 10 to 20 percent, would be more appropriate.

Pulling It All Together

By the time you're done, you should be able to project each of the following for each strategy in your plan by quarter:

_____ *strategy is projected to achieve the following outcomes by the* *end of quarter _____ with a _____ margin of error:*

- MROI of $TBD:$1
- MQLs of X
- SQLs of X
- Revenue generated from marketing leads of $X
- Gross profit generated from these leads of $X

Our client Sarah, a marketing director attendee at one of RedRover's three-day Marketing Results Guaranteed BootCamps, pulled it all together. Like many of her peers, she initially was daunted by the prospect of having her compensation tied to MROI projections. "The idea of my paycheck depending on marketing predictions makes me nauseous. It's like threading a needle with your eyes closed." That's a perfect summary of the anxiety many marketing leaders face when challenged with accurate forecasting.

As the BootCamp unfolded, however, Sarah's perspective began to shift. The session on leveraging historical channel performance combined with industry benchmarks to arrive at future predictions was a game changer. Sarah learned precisely how to mine her company's past marketing efforts for gold and recognized that this data was like being given a map to the past, allowing her to predict the future with a lot more confidence. Sarah grew confident in her ability to identify patterns and make educated projections about future outcomes. This approach demystified the process, transforming her trepidation into excitement about the opportunity to leverage research-backed projections for larger payouts.

The Power of Inspiration and Commitment in Achieving Guaranteed ROI

One of the foundational pillars of marketing is trust. Trust in the strategy, trust in the execution, and, most importantly, trust in the people behind it all. Trust, however, is a two-way street. While CEOs and marketing leaders place their trust in their teams, it's equally crucial for teams to trust their own predictions and capabilities. This trust becomes the catalyst for inspiration.

Why is inspiration so essential, especially when discussing ROI? The answer lies in the transformative power of inspired teams. An inspired team doesn't just work to meet expectations; it strives to exceed them. It views challenges not as setbacks but as opportunities for growth. It believes in the strategies it develops and stands unwaveringly behind its ROI projections. Inspiration fuels creativity, and creative teams produce creative content. This level of commitment and enthusiasm is not something that can be mandated or bought; it must be inspired. Inspired teams are fuelled by emotions, and these emotions filter down into the brand and its audience, generating more customer loyalty and positive customer experiences, all of which increase ROI.

Market Research as the Foundation for Inspiration

In marketing, knowledge isn't just power; it's the lifeblood of strategy. Market research, as discussed in Battle 3, is the bridge between your brand and its audience. It illuminates the needs, desires, pain points, and aspirations of your target market. By understanding these facets, you can craft strategies that resonate, engage, and convert.

But here's the real revolution: Market research doesn't just inform; it empowers. When your team is armed with concrete data, its projections aren't mere guesses. They are sophisticated predictions. And this confidence in the projections is what inspires your team to stand behind them.

> **WHEN YOUR TEAM IS ARMED WITH CONCRETE DATA, ITS PROJECTIONS AREN'T MERE GUESSES. THEY ARE INFORMED PREDICTIONS. THIS CONFIDENCE IN THE PROJECTIONS IS WHAT INSPIRES YOUR TEAM TO STAND BEHIND THEM.**

Leadership plays a pivotal role in cultivating a culture of inspiration. The environment in which a team operates can either stifle or stimulate inspiration. Inspirational leaders foster a culture of openness, where ideas are encouraged, failures are viewed as learning opportunities, and successes are collectively celebrated. They set the vision, rally the team, and ensure that the journey toward guaranteed ROI is as rewarding as the destination.

The Psychology of Commitment in ROI

The human psyche plays a pivotal role in marketing, particularly when it comes to ROI projections and commitments. The interplay between the mind's innate need for consistency and the external pressures of delivering on promises provides a fascinating lens through which you can understand the motivations and actions of marketers.

At the heart of this psychology lies the theory of cognitive dissonance, introduced by psychologist Leon Festinger in 1957. This theory asserts that individuals are driven by an intrinsic need to maintain consistency among their beliefs, values, and behaviors. When inconsistencies arise, creating dissonance, it leads to internal tension, prompting individuals to alleviate this discomfort.

In the marketing context, this tension manifests when there's a discrepancy between projected MROI and actual outcomes. Marketers, having pledged certain results, feel an innate drive to meet these targets due to both external pressures and this internal need for consistency.

> **MARKETERS, HAVING PLEDGED CERTAIN RESULTS, FEEL AN INNATE DRIVE TO MEET THESE TARGETS DUE TO BOTH EXTERNAL PRESSURES AND THIS INTERNAL NEED FOR CONSISTENCY.**

This is further underscored by neuroscientific studies, like "Neural Mechanisms of Cognitive Dissonance (Revised): An EEG Study" from the *Journal of Neuroscience*[34], which demonstrate that cognitive dissonance can lead to a decrease in ratings for rejected items, a phenomenon known as the spreading of alternatives. This effect plays a significant role in how marketers perceive and evaluate their decisions. When cognitive dissonance occurs—such as when a chosen marketing strategy underperforms—there's a tendency to devalue the rejected alternatives. This leads marketers to overvalue their current strategy despite evidence suggesting a need for change. Understanding this neural activity is crucial, as it can help marketers recognize and counteract potential biases in their strategic evaluations, ensuring more objective and effective decision-making processes.

CHECK OUT THE 12 BATTLES™ READER HUB at marketingtoolsforyou.com for this free resource:

COGNITIVE DISSONANCE DEEP DIVE

Commitment as a Double-Edged Sword

Committing to specific ROI projections acts as both a motivational catalyst and a potential source of stress. The act of publicly voicing a projection solidifies it in the marketer's mind, making it a tangible goal. This commitment, combined with the cognitive dissonance experienced when the goal isn't met, can drive teams to think creatively and optimize strategies.

However, overcommitting or setting unrealistic targets leads to undue stress and rushed decisions. The balance lies in making informed,

---

[34] Colosio, Marco, et al. "Neural Mechanisms of Cognitive Dissonance (Revised): An EEG Study." *Journal of Neuroscience*, vol. 37, no. 20, 17 May 2017, pp. 5074–5083, doi.org/10.1523/JNEUROSCI.3209-16.2017.

realistic commitments that challenge but don't overwhelm.

The Impact of External Commitments

While the internal drive for consistency is strong, external factors like stakeholder expectations magnify this effect. Public commitments to leadership teams or boards amplify the psychological weight of these commitments, adding motivation to deliver on them. Neuroscientifically, such external pressures can influence neural pathways related to decision making and stress response.[35]

Harnessing the Power of Commitment

To harness the psychology of commitment, marketers need self-awareness to recognize their cognitive biases and the desire for consistency that can influence decisions. They should view missed projections as learning opportunities that promote a growth mindset. Regular communication between marketers and their leaders can alleviate pressures of commitment, fostering trust. When significant external factors arise, such as notable economic shifts or aggressive new competition, be open to occasionally revisiting projections that your margin of error can't realistically cover.

Understanding the workings of the mind in the context of MROI is as crucial as understanding the market itself. Neuroscience provides deeper insight into the neural mechanisms behind these psychological processes, helping marketers harness the power of commitment to achieve better, more consistent results.

Leadership Strategies for Instilling Confidence in Your Team

Following are eight psychological strategies a CEO or marketing leader can employ to instill confidence in their team regarding their MROI projections:

---

[35] Id.

1. **Growth mindset encouragement:** Promote the belief that abilities can be developed through dedication and hard work. This fosters resilience and a love for learning, enabling team members to view challenges (like MROI projections) as opportunities to grow.

2. **Positive reinforcement:** Recognize and praise efforts, not just outcomes. This reinforces the desired behavior and encourages team members to trust their judgments and stand by their projections. Be careful though; in the end, your team does need to deliver outcomes.

3. **Visualization techniques:** Encourage team members to visualize successful outcomes. Imagining a positive result helps reduce anxiety and increase confidence in their projections. In a one-to-one meeting with each individual member of your marketing team, ask them to imagine what success looks like at the end of the year. If they were talking with friends about that success, how would they describe it? What's the impact on the rest of the team? How does the win make them feel?

4. **Cognitive reframing:** Teach the team to reframe negative thoughts or doubts. Instead of "What if my projection is wrong?" encourage "What can I learn from this projection, whether it's right or wrong?"

5. **Anchoring past successes:** Regularly remind your team of past successes, emphasizing that the team has overcome challenges and made accurate projections before and can do so again.

6. **Team cohesion activities:** Organize team-building exercises to foster trust and understanding among team members. A united team is more likely to stand confidently behind collective decisions.

7. **Affirmation practices:** Encourage team members to use affirmations. Repeatedly affirming one's abilities can instill confidence. For example: "I am capable of making accurate ROI projections."

8. **Feedback loop:** Create an environment where feedback, both positive and constructive, is regularly shared. Knowing where they stand and having clarity on areas of improvement helps team members trust their capabilities and work on their weaknesses.

By leveraging these psychological strategies, leaders can tap into their team's intrinsic motivators.

The path to guaranteed outcomes is not just about predicting MROI; it's about inspiring teams to confidently stand behind their projections. Inspiration, paired with knowledge, is the true catalyst for guaranteed success.

Battle 12 Research Insights[36]

35% of survey respondents strongly agree that their marketing team has a high level of accountability to achieving specific marketing outcomes. Given what's at stake, that number has a lot of room for improvement. Forty-nine percent agree, leaving 16 percent that are neutral, disagree, or are unsure.

Success Story

BrightPath Software[37], a mid-sized enterprise in the SaaS industry, faced significant challenges in its marketing outcomes the first half

---

[36] From the "2024 RedRover U.S. Middle-Market B2B Marketing Performance Study," available in the 12 Battles™ Reader Hub at marketingtoolsforyou.com.
[37] Client details have been modified to respect confidentiality.

of its fiscal year. Backed by a private equity group, underperformance was not an option. The head of marketing, Stephen, reached out to RedRover about our GO Plan service. Our research team took quick action to rapidly execute a market research protocol that would allow us to arrive at a predictable strategy.

This in-depth analysis revealed a feasible target of a $5:$1 MROI and $900,000 in incremental sales, which we confidently guaranteed over the next year of our partnership.

Three quarters into execution of the BrightPath plan, the company faced unexpected market shifts due to a major industry innovation causing us to miss that quarter's projections by a mile. RedRover quickly spearheaded a strategy recalibration as a result. Instead of encountering frustration, the proactive approach was met with enthusiasm by BrightPath's CEO. He actively engaged in the strategic pivot, working hand-in-hand with his team and ours. This collaborative effort and positive energy, fueled by the CEO's eagerness to support the turnaround, was instrumental in exceeding the projected $900,000 in incremental sales by more than $100,000 due to an overperforming fourth quarter. This success story exemplifies the impact of adaptive strategy and the powerful role of a supportive, hands-on leadership style in navigating market challenges.

Cautionary Tale

EfficientEnergy[38], a $34M renewable energy firm, engaged RedRover for our GO Plan service of market research and strategy building, seeking to boost its market presence. While our analysis resulted in a projected $4:$1 MROI that we guaranteed and would have resulted in $750,000 in incremental sales from its maximum marketing budget, the company's president was set on achieving $1.25M in

---

[38] Client details have been modified to respect confidentiality.

growth *without* increasing the budget. While RedRover did not guarantee that ambitious goal, instead standing behind the original $750,000 sales goal, the well-intended president chose to move forward regardless, hoping to attain it due to pressure from his board. The RedRover team worked alongside EfficientEnergy's internal team in executing the strategy.

The internal team, under the weight of these inflated expectations, felt immense pressure and morale dropped notably. Despite everyone's efforts, the campaign only achieved $690,000 of the initial $750,000 projection (a far cry from the $1.25M that the president desired) due, in part, to turnover among EfficientEnergy's internal team. The disparity between the president's goal and the actual outcome created a sense of defeat among team members leading to significant turnover within the marketing department. The president was disappointed by the turnover and took responsibility for the outcomes. The experience notably changed how he looked at goal setting and his role as inspirational champion for his team. This case highlights the importance of setting realistic goals based on data-driven insights and considering the impact of such decisions on team morale and retention.

> **START A REVOLUTION: INSPIRE YOUR TEAM TO STAND BEHIND THEIR MROI PROJECTIONS.**

BATTLE ARMOR: TOOLS AND RESOURCES FOR LEVERAGE

My mission is to help you create a high-performance, predictable marketing plan that allows you to realize your vision for growth. With the right approach, you can make marketing an unbeatable competitive advantage and conquer much larger rivals. This pursuit to balance the playing field is more than professional—it's personal. Helping your company thrive is how I honor my father's legacy and support leaders like him. My exclusive 12 Battles™ Reader Hub offers every resource available in this book to add to your arsenal. I call these tools "battle armor" because they are designed to shield your business from competitive threats and prepare you to win on the battlefield. Access all of these tactical assets at marketingtoolsforyou.com. Be sure to sign up there to receive email notifications when new tools are added.

CHAPTERS	BATTLE ARMOR RESOURCES
Preface	12 Battles™ Framework Downloadable Card
Preface	12 Battles™ Framework Readiness Assessment
Introduction	2024 RedRover U.S. Middle-Market B2B Marketing Performance Study
Battle 1	Agency "Leveling Up" Script
Battle 2	Survey Questions for 10 Customer Insights
Battle 2	Market Research Firm Vetting Guide
Battle 3	Internal Stakeholder Interview Guide Template
Battle 3	External Stakeholder Interview Guide Template

CHAPTERS	BATTLE ARMOR RESOURCES
Battle 3	Competitive Intelligence Platforms
Battle 3	Competitive Index
Battle 3	Value Proposition Comparison Grid
Battle 3	Ascending Offer Strategy Inventory
Battle 3	Sales and Marketing Alignment Inventory
Battle 3	Sales Process/People/Comp Plan Evaluation Best Practices
Battle 3	Marketing Performance Audit Template
Battle 3	Customer Transaction Analysis Template
Battle 3	Sample Size Calculator
Battle 3	Survey Length Estimation Calculator
Battle 3	Survey Questionnaire Template
Battle 4	MROI Calculator
Battle 4	Industry Specific MROI Targets
Battle 4	Attribution Model Assessment
Battle 4	Attribution Modeling Platforms
Battle 5	Brandscape Template
Battle 6	20 Questions to Ask Agency Contenders
Battle 8	War Room Strategy Debate Customer Journey Pre-Read
Battle 8	War Room Strategy Debate Email Template
Battle 8	War Room Strategy Debate Top 10 Questions
Battle 8	War Room Strategy Debate Facilitation Guide
Battle 8	War Room Strategy Debate Printable Team Agenda

CHAPTERS	BATTLE ARMOR RESOURCES
Battle 8	War Room Strategy Vetting Worksheet
Battle 9	Optimization Meeting Editable Agendas
Battle 9	Optimization Meeting Facilitation Guide
Battle 9	Monthly Optimization Meeting Excel Worksheet
Battle 10	Agency vs. Internal Team Comparison Guide
Battle 10	20 Questions to Ask Agency Contenders
Battle 10	Internal Pay-for-Performance Models
Battle 11	Guide for Calculating Average Customer Lifespan
Battle 11	Guide for Calculating Accurate CAC Metric
Battle 11	Top Dashboard Platforms
Battle 11	Marketing SOP Template
Battle 12	Cognitive Dissonance Deep Dive

PARTING WORDS

As I put the finishing touches on this labor of love, I want to celebrate you and your openness to making revolutionary changes within your company. It takes courage to go the road less traveled, but that's the reason why marketing can become your sustainable competitive advantage. Most companies don't know how or aren't willing to put in the work required to generate predictable marketing outcomes. My deepest hope is to not overwhelm you but to inspire you to stop settling for less than you deserve.

I'm honored to be a part of your journey to predictable growth. I want to see the weight of company performance be less of a burden, giving you the freedom to enjoy the company to which you have given your blood, sweat, and tears. In fact, I'd be delighted to celebrate with you. There's a link in the 12 Battles™ Reader Hub that's designed just for that purpose. Look for the Celebration link and share your successes with me. And remember, you're not in this alone. The entire pack and I at RedRover are here to support and serve you—whatever you may need.

GLOSSARY

12 Battles™ Framework: A proprietary methodology of RedRover Sales & Marketing Strategy for developing and executing a results-guaranteed marketing plan, leveraging intensive market research coupled with a powerful strategic planning effort.

12 Battles™ Readiness Assessment: An evaluative tool designed by RedRover Sales & Marketing Strategy to measure a company's preparedness for implementing the 12 Battles™ Framework and adopting results-guaranteed marketing strategies.

2024 RedRover U.S. Middle-Market B2B Marketing Performance Study: A significant research study sponsored by RedRover Sales & Marketing Strategy, focusing on the marketing performance and KPIs of middle-market B2B companies in the U.S.

ABM (Account-Based Marketing) Strategy: A strategic approach in B2B marketing focused on targeting specific accounts or customer segments through hyper-personalized marketing touch-points interspersed with complementary sales outreach.

A/B Testing: A marketing experiment where the audience is split into two groups to test variations of a campaign in an effort to determine which one performs better. Version A of the marketing content is shown to one half of the audience and version B to the other half. Campaign elements that can be tested include headlines, content, images/graphics, audience segmentation, calls to action, etc.

Advertising Optimization: Enhancing advertising campaigns for better performance and MROI.

Affiliate and Influencer Marketing: Marketing strategies that involve promoting products through affiliates or influencers who receive compensation for their efforts.

Alignment: Ensuring consistency and direction in business strategies and objectives.

Allocation: Distributing resources, such as budget or time, to various tasks or projects.

Analytics and Reporting: The process of measuring, analyzing, and reporting marketing performance to understand effectiveness and MROI.

Ascending Offer Strategy: A sequence of offers that increase in value, complexity, or commitment designed to encourage a customer to increase their investment after experiencing a company or brand.

Attribution: Assigning credit for a sale or conversion to a specific marketing touchpoint.

Attribution Modeling: Analyzing which touchpoints receive credit for conversions.

Awareness Stage: The first stage of the customer buying journey where potential customers become aware of a product or service.

B2B: Business-to-business transactions or marketing; businesses that sell or market to other businesses as compared to end consumers.

B2C: Business-to-consumer transactions or marketing; businesses that sell or market to end consumers as compared to other businesses.

Backlink: A link from one website pointing to another.

Brandscape: A visual or conceptual landscape of a brand's position in the market and, as such, a combination of the words "brand" and "landscape."

CAC (Customer Acquisition Cost): The expense incurred to acquire a new customer.

Campaign Analysis: Examining the effectiveness of a specific marketing campaign.

Campaign Metrics: Quantitative measurements to evaluate campaign performance.

Competitive Index: A measurement of a company's competitive position in the market.

Consideration Stage: The stage in the customer buying journey where potential customers consider different solutions.

Content Engagement Metrics: Measurements of user interaction with content, such as time on page and social shares.

Conversion Stage: The customer journey stage where potential customers decide to purchase.

Custom Attribution Model: An attribution model that incorporates data from multiple touchpoints and assigns credit based on specific criteria; weights are customized for each touchpoint based on the nuances of the customer journey in that specific industry.

Customer Insights: Deep understanding or findings about customers' behaviors and preferences.

Customer Journey: The path customers take from first learning about a product or service to purchase and all of the touchpoints along the way.

Customer Transaction Analysis: Analyzing historical customer transaction data to uncover trends, profitable segments, and customer buying behaviors.

Data-Driven Attribution: A method to allocate credit to various marketing touchpoints using machine learning via Google Analytics.

Email Marketing: The use of email to promote products or services and develop relationships with potential customers.

Engagement: The degree to which customers interact with a brand, content, or an ad.

Event Marketing: The process of promoting a product, brand, or service through in-person or virtual events.

First-Touch Attribution: Allocating marketing credit to the first touchpoint in the customer journey.

Google Ads: Google's online advertising platform.

Google Analytics: A web analytics service offered by Google that tracks and reports website traffic.

Google Tag Manager: A tag management system that allows for quick and easy updates to tracking tags and code snippets on a website or mobile app.

GO Plan: RedRover Sales & Marketing Strategy's signature Growth Optimization planning service, which includes deep market research that informs a tailored and results-guaranteed marketing strategy.

Gross Profit: Total profit before deducting operating expenses.

Incrementality Testing: Evaluating the incremental impact of specific marketing channels on overall performance.

Influencers: Individuals who have the power to affect purchase decisions because of their authority, knowledge, or relationship with their audience.

Insights: Actionable findings derived from data analysis.

Interactive Content: Quizzes, polls, and similar tools used in digital marketing to engage the audience in a conversational way.

Jim Collins: The author of *Great By Choice* and a speaker known for his research on business sustainability and growth.

KPIs (Key Performance Indicators): Metrics used to evaluate the success of an organization or activity.

Last-Touch Attribution: Assigning marketing credit to the final touchpoint before conversion.

Linear Attribution: Distributing marketing credit evenly across all touchpoints in the customer journey.

LTV (Lifetime Value): Measures the average financial worth of a customer over their entire engagement with a business; it is calculated as average annual gross profit per customer x average lifespan of a customer in years.

LTV:CAC Ratio: A key marketing efficiency indicator measuring the relationship between the lifetime value of a customer and the cost of acquiring that customer.

Marketing Clarity Assessment: A marketing performance audit conducted by the RedRover Sales & Marketing Strategy team that gives CEOs and marketing leaders clarity into the performance of their current marketing plan.

Marketing Dashboard: A tool for CEOs and marketing leaders to monitor key marketing metrics and insights for making MROI-driven decisions.

Marketing Performance Audit: A comprehensive analysis of a company's marketing strategy performance by comparing it against industry benchmarks and past performance.

Marketing Results Guaranteed BootCamp: A 3-day, 18-hour intensive course led by the RedRover Sales & Marketing Strategy team that gives CEOs and marketing leaders the knowledge and skills to launch their own market research protocol and develop their own research-backed marketing strategy to drive high performance and predictable outcomes.

Marketing Results Guaranteed MasterMind: A weekly peer group of B2B leaders led by the RedRover Sales & Marketing Strategy team that offers education, coaching, and accountability to support the development and launch of research-backed marketing strategies that drive predictable outcomes.

Market Shifts: Changes in market dynamics, such as consumer behavior or competitor movements.

Market Trends: Patterns or movements in the market over time.

Middle-Market Companies: Businesses with annual revenues between $10M and $1B. Lower middle-market companies are those with revenue between $10M and $150M and identified as the most responsive to the 12 Battles™ Framework.

MQL (Marketing Qualified Lead): A lead that has engaged with company marketing efforts and is deemed to be more likely to make a purchase than other leads.

MROI (Marketing ROI): A crucial metric in the 12 Battles™ Framework used to assess the profitability of marketing investments; it is calculated as (New Sales Generated - Marketing Costs) / Marketing Costs.

Mystery Shopping: A process of evaluating competitors anonymously to assess customer experience and overall offering.

Offer Strategy Evaluation: An assessment to compare a company's offer strategy to those of its competitors based on both customers' needs and desires and competitors' offers.

Optimization: Improving processes or strategies for better efficiency or outcome including challenging and re-evaluating every campaign element to ensure optimal performance.

Paid Advertising: The use of paid strategies to send marketing messages to target audiences, including PPC and display ads.

Post-Purchase Stage: The customer journey stage after customers make a purchase, focusing on retention and advocacy.

PPC (Pay-Per-Click) Advertising: Internet advertising model used to drive traffic to websites, in which an advertiser pays a publisher when the ad is clicked.

Predictive Validation: Using attribution models to forecast future marketing outcomes and comparing these predictions to actual results.

Qualitative Research: Stakeholder interviews, competitive surveillance, value proposition and offer strategy comparisons, etc. used to determine the scope of beliefs about a brand and its place in the market (must be vetted using statistically valid quantitative research).

Quantitative Research: The hard numbers from marketing performance audits, customer transaction analysis, customer and prospect surveys, etc. that statistically validate or invalidate the perceptions, opinions, and viewpoints derived from qualitative research.

RedRover Sales & Marketing Strategy: One of the only full-service B2B-focused marketing agencies in the U.S. that offers guaranteed MROI.

Results-Driven Culture: An organizational focus on achieving specific outcomes.

ROI (Return on Investment): Measuring the profitability of an investment.

SaaS (Software as a Service): Software provided on a subscription basis.

Sales and Marketing Alignment Inventory: An assessment tool to evaluate the synchronization and effectiveness of sales and marketing teams.

Sales Cycle: The process from the first contact with a potential customer to the final sale.

Scalability: In marketing, it is the ability to maintain at or above the current level of marketing performance as marketing investment increases.

Scorecards: Tools used to track and measure performance against defined metrics.

Segmentation: Dividing a market into distinct groups based on specific criteria.

SEO (Search Engine Optimization): The practice of increasing the quantity and quality of traffic to a website through organic (unpaid) search engine results.

Social Media Management: The process of managing online interactions and content across social media platforms.

SOPs (Standard Operating Procedures): A set of step-by-step instructions to perform specific tasks.

SQL (Sales Qualified Lead): A lead that has engaged with more advanced company content (e.g., case studies, pricing details, product comparisons) and is believed to have buying intent.

Stakeholders: Individuals or groups with an interest in a company's actions or outcomes.

Stakeholder Interviews: A research methodology to see where stakeholder views and perspectives align and differ and to identify the boundaries of hypotheses and perspectives that will be vetted against a statistically valid audience.

Time-Decay Attribution: Assigning marketing credit to touchpoints that are closer to the conversion event while gradually reducing the credit assigned to earlier interactions.

Touchpoint: Any point of interaction between a business and its customers.

Upselling: Encouraging customers to buy a higher-end product or add-on.

User-Generated Content: Content created and shared by users or customers, fostering community and peer-to-peer learning.

USPs (Unique Selling Points): Features that differentiate a product from its competitors.

Value Proposition Comparison Grid: A tool to compare a company's value proposition against those of competitors across various factors.

War Room Strategy Debate: A focused, no-holds-barred session designed to dissect, challenge, and fortify marketing plans, ensuring that every aspect of the strategy is battle-tested and ready to conquer the market.

ABOUT THE AUTHOR

Lori Turner-Wilson: Visionary CEO, Renowned Author, Powerhouse Speaker, and Marketing Battle Leader

Lori Turner-Wilson isn't just at the helm of RedRover Sales & Marketing Strategy as its CEO and co-founder; she's a trailblazer who is reshaping the landscape of business marketing. With a storied career spanning more than three decades, Lori has been pivotal in crafting and delivering marketing strategies that yield measurable and substantial results. Her leadership has propelled RedRover to a distinguished position as one of the only full-service B2B marketing firms in the U.S. with the courage to offer a true marketing ROI guarantee to its clients, thus earning the firm the moniker: "The Results-Guaranteed Agency."

Since founding RedRover in 2006, Lori has dedicated herself to refining a methodology that leverages in-depth market research to forge marketing strategies that are not only effective and efficient but also ensure predictable outcomes. This methodology, known as the 12 Battles™ Framework, has been the cornerstone for countless companies, providing them with a powerful arsenal for success. And now, in her seminal work—her latest international best-selling book, *The B2B Marketing Revolution™: A Battle Plan for Guaranteed Marketing Outcomes*—she reveals to CEOs and marketing leaders her philosophy and her revolutionary approach to guaranteeing MROI. Lori is driven by a profound commitment to bolster middle-market companies by devising marketing strategies that provide them with the necessary tools and insights to effectively compete with much larger enterprises. Her efforts aim to close the strategic and resource divide that often places smaller companies at a disadvantage, ensuring they too can realize strong returns on their marketing investments.

Her formative experiences in Fortune 1000 marketing sparked a realization that changed her professional trajectory. In these enterprise leadership roles, she had the opportunity to hire many of the top 10 marketing agencies in the country, only to find out they lacked the desire to take accountability for metrics that actually matter— such as incremental gross profit. Dragging these agencies into peak performance was agonizing.

Lori envisioned an agency that cared as much about the bottom line as she did—one that could move nimbly and effect the growth trajectory of a company rapidly and efficiently by building strategy on a backbone of comprehensive market research. She realized that she should build what she couldn't find and raise the bar in the industry that she loved along the way. So, in 2006, RedRover Sales & Marketing Strategy was born. And it continues to revolutionize the traditional, obsolete marketing-agency model.

Lori's unwavering commitment to guaranteed outcomes has not only changed the growth trajectory of countless companies, but it has also garnered RedRover numerous accolades, including being named one of the "Top 10 Companies to Watch" by the Greater Memphis Chamber and one of the "Best Places to Work" by the *Memphis Business Journal*. Lori also received the "Vistage CEO Impact Award" from her peers in the Vistage CEO network for her contributions to other Vistage peers and for her work to leverage Vistage principles to grow RedRover into an industry-leading marketing agency.

The B2B Marketing Revolution™ is Lori's third best-selling book in the field of marketing. She penned the Amazon best seller *W.O.O.F.— Why Ordinary Organizations Fail* in 2016 and served as a contributing ghostwriter in 2008 on the best seller *The Complete Idiot's Guide*© *to Guerrilla Marketing.*

Lori's dedication to RedRover is more than just business—it's a personal crusade to elevate middle-market companies, allowing them to assert their rightful place in the market. With the recent national expansion of RedRover, her strategic insights are now igniting market potential and championing profitability from coast to coast. Her leadership, inspired by her father's entrepreneurial journey, is setting a new standard for marketing success on a national scale.

www.ingramcontent.com/pod-product-compliance
Lightning Source LLC
Chambersburg PA
CBHW052110030426

42335CB00025B/2911